Paganism

Unlocking the Secrets of Druidism and Norse Spirituality for Beginners

© Copyright 2023 - All rights reserved.

The content contained within this book may not be reproduced, duplicated, or transmitted without direct written permission from the author or the publisher.

Under no circumstances will any blame or legal responsibility be held against the publisher, or author, for any damages, reparation, or monetary loss due to the information contained within this book, either directly or indirectly.

Legal Notice:

This book is copyright protected. It is only for personal use. You cannot amend, distribute, sell, use, quote, or paraphrase any part, or the content within this book, without the consent of the author or publisher.

Disclaimer Notice:

Please note the information contained within this document is for educational and entertainment purposes only. All effort has been executed to present accurate, up-to-date, reliable, and complete information. No warranties of any kind are declared or implied. Readers acknowledge that the author is not engaging in the rendering of legal, financial, medical, or professional advice. The content within this book has been derived from various sources. Please consult a licensed professional before attempting any techniques outlined in this book.

By reading this document, the reader agrees that under no circumstances is the author responsible for any losses, direct or indirect, that are incurred as a result of the use of the information contained within this document, including, but not limited to, errors, omissions, or inaccuracies.

Free Bonus from Silvia Hill available for limited time

Hi Spirituality Lovers!

My name is Silvia Hill, and first off, I want to THANK YOU for reading my book.

Now you have a chance to join my exclusive spirituality email list so you can get the ebooks below for free as well as the potential to get more spirituality ebooks for free! Simply click the link below to join.

P.S. Remember that it's 100% free to join the list.

$27 FREE BONUSES

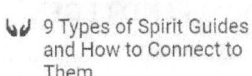
9 Types of Spirit Guides and How to Connect to Them

How to Develop Your Intuition: 7 Secrets for Psychic Development and Tarot Reading

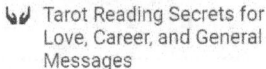
Tarot Reading Secrets for Love, Career, and General Messages

Access your free bonuses here
https://livetolearn.lpages.co/paganism-paperback/

Table of Contents

PART 1: DRUIDISM FOR BEGINNERS 1
  INTRODUCTION 2
  CHAPTER 1: CELTS AND DRUIDS: HOW DO THEY CONNECT? 4
  CHAPTER 2: ANCIENT VS. MODERN DRUIDISM 12
  CHAPTER 3: DRUIDRY BASICS I: BELIEFS, WORLDS, AND TREASURES 22
  CHAPTER 4: DRUIDRY BASICS II: NATURE, CYCLES, AND SEASONS 32
  CHAPTER 5: DRUIDRY BASICS III: MYTHS AND LEGENDS 40
  CHAPTER 6: THE DRUID'S TOOLKIT 50
  CHAPTER 7: WORKING WITH THE AWEN 57
  CHAPTER 8: THE OGHAM AND TREE MAGIC 65
  CHAPTER 9: DRUIDIC RITUALS AND CEREMONIES 74
  CHAPTER 10: GROVE OR HEDGE? WALKING THE PATH IN THE MODERN DAY 82
  CONCLUSION 91
PART 2: NORSE SPIRITUALITY 93
  INTRODUCTION 94
  CHAPTER 1: THE OLD NORSE RELIGION 96
  CHAPTER 2: PANTHEON AND COSMOLOGY 105
  CHAPTER 3: DEATH AND THE AFTERLIFE 113
  CHAPTER 4: ASATRU VS. HEATHENRY 121
  CHAPTER 5: SEIÐR MAGIC AND SHAMANISM 130

CHAPTER 6: WORKING WITH THE GODDESS FREYJA 138
CHAPTER 7: JOURNEYING THROUGH YGGDRASILL 146
CHAPTER 8: NORSE RUNES 101 .... *155*
CHAPTER 9: RUNIC DIVINATION AND MAGIC 172
CHAPTER 10: GALDR MAGIC 180
CONCLUSION 188
GLOSSARY: NORSE TERMS 190
HERE'S ANOTHER BOOK BY SILVIA HILL THAT YOU MIGHT LIKE 197
FREE BONUS FROM SILVIA HILL AVAILABLE FOR LIMITED TIME 198
REFERENCES 199

Part 1: Druidism for Beginners

An Essential Guide to Druidry and Everything You Need to Know about Druid Magic, Solitary Druids, and Celtic Spirituality

Introduction

Druidry is a spiritual practice that touches three of our deepest desires - unleashing and expressing our full creative capacities, attuning ourselves and communicating with nature, and obtaining the keys to great knowledge and wisdom. These desires come from the three aspects of our being. These are often symbolized as the Singer, the Shaman, and the Sage. Practicing Druidry allows you to nurture the creative source within you, whether it wishes to emerge as a storyteller, painter, sculptor, or singer. It helps you stimulate the Shaman within you. The Shaman is the healing aspect. It is the lover and the appreciator of nature. Finally, it aims to cultivate your inner intellect and wisdom. This is the Sage that lies deep within all of us.

All the modern manifestations of Druidism ultimately aim to expand on the beliefs of ancient Druids. Ancient Druids are believed to be the guardians of this religious and magical tradition that dates back to pre-Christianity. This book starts off by discussing who the Celts and the Druids were. You'll find out why the Celtic culture and Druidry are so profoundly associated. When reading this book, you can expect to learn the differences and similarities between the ancient and modern druids. You'll understand how Druidry was revived and whether it was a genuine revival of ancient Druidry or just a limited adaptation of the practice.

You can also expect to learn about the primary Druidic beliefs, values, and theories on cosmology. You will learn everything you need to know regarding their beliefs about the world and creation. You will understand the basic principles of Druidism, the Four Sacred Treasures of the Celts, and the differences between the druidic "branches." This book will delve into the concept of the Wheel of the Year and the Sabbats. Then, you'll read about the numerous myths and legends that play a significant role in the life of modern druids and the Celts.

The best thing about this guide to Druidism is that it includes hands-on methods that will make your journey as a beginner a lot easier. For instance, you'll come across a comprehensive Druid toolkit that covers everything a modern druid needs to hold rituals and practice Druidic philosophy. You will find step-by-step instructions on how to create some of these tools yourself.

Most importantly, you will learn about the significance of trees in Druidic practices. There's an entire chapter that offers several steps and methods to spiritually connect and work with trees. It includes several practical and easy exercises you can do to prepare yourself for more intense tree magic practices. You'll also learn about Tree Astrology and find out what your tree sign and personality are according to ancient Druidic astrology.

This guide also delves into more intricate Druidic rituals and ceremonies. You'll come across the most common rituals held by modern Druids, along with their most popular celebrations. You will learn how to set up your own ritual or ceremony and gain insight into navigating your journey as a modern Druid.

Chapter 1: Celts and Druids: How Do They Connect?

Celtic culture has attracted the curiosity of a massive number of people throughout the world thanks to their Druidic rituals and traditions. However, most people are still relatively new to this topic and often get confused between Celts and Druids. While many people and even some literature misinterpret Druids and Celts as the same, they are actually separate people.

Celtic Mythology Symbol.
https://pixabay.com/photos/triskele-stone-drawing-rock-stone-52542/

The ancient Celtic culture started from different tribes residing in western and central Europe from 700 BCE to 400 CE. These tribes shared a common language, culture, and religion. Thus, this group was given the name Celts by ancient historians. The tribes later migrated to various parts of the world and took their language and culture with them. Although most of these tribes were scattered across the globe, they shared a common language, culture, art, religion, modes of warfare, and burial practices. Even though the rise of the roman empire absorbed most of the Celtic culture from major territories, it still remained prevalent in remote parts of Europe, including Britain and Ireland, where it is still practiced.

On the other hand, the Druids are a class of highly educated Celtic people. This class includes doctors, philosophers, poets, mathematicians, and spiritual leaders. They were considered an elite group of the Celtic society and were a legacy with mysterious abilities and extensive knowledge. Just like Celtic culture, Druidism remained and evolved over time. Today, Druids are associated with magic, wizardry, and spiritualism. In short, Celts and Druids are not the same, and while all Druids are Celts by origin, not all Celts are Druids by nature.

To further clarify your understanding of the Celts and Druids, this chapter will act as an introductory lesson to the Celtic culture, how it connects to Druidism, and the complete history of their evolution.

The Celtic Culture

The Celtic culture mainly consisted of its unique language. Other cultural features varied significantly across the different tribes. All of these tribes were collectively given the name "Celts," which many people consider to be a problematic label considering the tribes were not part of a unified state. In fact, they were so scattered that there weren't many common features. Moreover, the tribes weren't in direct contact with one another, and they lived quite a distance from each other. The Celtic culture spread and evolved with time. It changed most dramatically during the European iron age, as it was a period of cultural interaction and frequent migrations.

Most scholars suggest that the Celtic culture originated from three overlapping cultural groups closely related to one another. Each of these groups had a prominent cultural feature merged into Celtic culture. The first one of these groups, known as the Urnfield, was present during the late Bronze age. Their name was derived from cremating their dead, storing the remains in urns, and burying them. Although there's a lack of archeological knowledge proving the existence of these people, this culture was later adopted by other tribes moving forward. The bronze age preceded the iron age, when ironworking technology became widespread throughout the world, replacing the use of bronze.

The second group that merged to form the Celtic culture included the Hallstatt culture, which was named after a site in Upper Austria where the tribe resided. This culture evolved and spread across the continent, including Switzerland, Austria, Germany, France, and Bohemia. Thus, the western part of this region is where the ancient Celts first originated. The expansion of this culture throughout Europe was likely through trade, intermarriages, tribal alliances, and migration. This generation of Celtic tribes prospered through abundant local salt, iron, and copper deposits. These commodities were traded along the waterways and kept them adrift and migrating. Their trade reached the Mediterranean cultures, evidenced by the presence of gold and amber jewelry present in the Hallstatt burial mounds. This culture died out at the beginning of the 5th century BCE, probably due to the shortage of resources or increased tribal competition.

The third cultural group that contributed to the making of the Celtic culture is the La Tène culture, which was named after a site in Switzerland. This group of tribes was extremely diverse in every sense, with similarities lying only in art, religion, and language. The La Tène culture spanned western and central Europe, from Ireland to Romania. Cultural features of this generation of Celtic individuals included ironworking, vegetal designs, swirling-styled art, offerings made in water, and weapon deposition in tombs. Many of these features were prevalent in the overall Celtic culture and, thus, made up a large part of the cultural features.

Celtics in Spain vs. Britain

As you now know, there were multiple tribes collectively known as the Celts, including the Britons, Gauls, Irish, Galatians, and Gaels. Two tribes, the Galatians and the Britons, were the most prominent in establishing the basis of the Celtic culture.

The Galatians resided in the Asturias region, now included in the area of northern Spain. This tribe had successfully fought off invasion attempts from the Romans and the Moors, the latter being successful in invading nearby regions and thus ruling much of current-day southern Spain. Galatian traditions make up a considerable part of Celtic events and rituals and hold evidence of Celtic influence. Cultural features of the Galatian tribe greatly resembled Celtic culture, with similarities mostly in ancient art and symbols. For instance, many descendants of the Galatian tribes still partake in ancient dances accompanied by bagpipes, a musical instrument often associated with Celtic culture, more commonly observed in Ireland and Scotland Celtic culture. Moreover, their regional flag is adorned by a symbol similar to the Celtic cross.

On the other hand, the Britons and Gauls initially settled in the northwestern part of France, which is known today as Brittany. What makes this tribe unique and such a massive part of today's Celtic culture is that they managed to retain most of the Celts' cultural features because they were located at an isolated site and thus avoided most attacks. Many festivals now celebrated there can be traced back to Celtic origins. Initially, the Romans did not manage to invade the Britons but later succeeded, pushing them to an island near Wales and Cornwall and another north of Scotland.

Celtic Religion and Society

Another common characteristic among the group of tribes known as the Celts were their religion and societal norms. The Celts had a polytheistic belief in various gods associated with various aspects of life. However, the knowledge regarding the exact details of their religion is limited to the works of classical authors, as the Celts themselves did not leave any religious descriptions. Although there were many variations across different regions and evolved over time, some common features of the ancient Celtic culture include:

- Votive offerings were dedicated to different gods to ask for blessings. The offerings included sacrificed animals, weapons, and food items
- The consideration of sacred groves, rivers, springs, and other natural sites as being referenced
- A belief in the afterlife, thus, depositing of valuables and everyday goods in the deceased's tombs
- A strong belief in the protective powers of totems, taboos, and sacrifices
- Religious ceremonies led by Druids and pagans

The Druids were not particularly fond of committing their knowledge to writing, so there isn't written evidence of the Celtic religion's sacred texts, prayers, or hymns. There were some mentions of key gods with all-embracing powers, including Cernunnos, who represented fertility and nature, and Lugus, who represented the sun. Lugus, also known as Lugh in later periods, was a major figure in the Celtic religion and was perhaps the only universally worshiped being across the various Celtic tribes. There was also Sequana, a female goddess associated with the rivers and healing springs, and the goddess Epona who was associated with horses.

Another unusual characteristic of the Celtic religion that sets them apart is that most of their gods were viewed as trios. Each entity represented a different aspect of the same divinity, thus forming a trio. For instance, the three mother goddesses of the Celtic religion were a famous trinity. Each of the Matronae represents power, strength, and fertility, respectively. There were numerous other local and regional gods and goddesses, most of whom were associated with matters of primary concern and everyday life. These involved healing, hunting, tribal identity, warfare, sovereignty, and protection. The Celtic religion had a distinct identity from other cultures. Still, after the invasions and merging of different tribes, Greek and Roman culture strongly influenced Celtic religion. The sacred Celtic sites began to use larger stone temples instead of simply being surrounded by earthworks. At this time, the Greco-Roman gods were incorporated into the Celtic culture.

The absence of first-hand written records makes it challenging to pinpoint the exact situation of the Celtic society back in the day. Still, from what was found, it can be concluded that the ancient Celtic society was hierarchical in nature. Most Celtic tribes followed this hierarchical system which maintained stability in the society. The top class consisted of the rulers and elite warriors. This population was limited and considered to be high society. Next in line were the religious leaders and the Druids. The Druids were considered living repositories of the Celtic community's collected knowledge. They were also believed to be an elite class and were very well respected in society. They were also exempt from paying taxes or partaking in military service. Finally, there was the specialized workforce of the society. These included craft workers, farmers, traders, and slaves. This was the largest group of the society and mostly comprised rural or agrarian individuals.

In the beginning, the tribes themselves were ruled by monarchs, but with time, the ruling system changed to elected chiefs and officials. Some tribes also had a small council of elders that was responsible for making the ruling decisions of the society. Two or more separate Celtic tribes would often merge for mutual assistance and development. This would result in one or both tribes depending on one another for resources. Joining tribes was mainly done due to the looming threat of the Romans. So, by the end of this period, there were many confederations of tribes of the Celts.

Another fascinating fact about the Celtic society was the treatment of women. There is evidence that there were multiple women chiefs in Celtic Britain and many female monarchs who were responsible for not just ruling powerful tribes but also leading them into battle. The women were also treated equally regarding burial ground offerings, as evidence proves that the same amount of goods was buried for both men and women of certain Celtic tribes.

The Origin of Druidism

As you know, Druids were considered an essential part of the Celtic community and sought out for wisdom and knowledge. They had accumulated knowledge of the whole Celtic culture throughout history. Thus, they were extremely valuable assets and were treated as such. The word Druid is composed of both Latin and Gaulish words, "Druidae" and "Druides," respectively. The word can be broken down into two Celtic words, "dru" and "wid," which means tree and wisdom. The world reflects the importance of trees in Celtic spiritualism and society. The word also translates to magician and sorcerer, which is what Druids were considered to be in the Celtic society.

There was a history of evolution in the Druidic society and the Celtic society's development. A total of four historical periods were observed that contributed to the major developmental phases of the Druids. First, there was the prehistoric period when the Celtic tribes moved to Ireland and Britain as the climate changed. The Druids in this period had extensive knowledge of astronomy, mathematics, and excellent engineering skills. During this period, the historical sites of Stonehenge and Newgrange were designed and built due to the excellent skills of these druids.

Unlike the rest of Celtic history, the next period was somewhat documented by classical writers. The texts of this period specifically mentioned the notable contributions of the Druids, who were divided into three major professions during this phase. These included the bards,

Druids with cultured knowledge of the songs and stories of various Celtic tribes, the Ovates, Druids with healing abilities and spiritual powers, and the Druids. They were philosophers, teachers, poets, and judges. The emergence of Christianity marked the beginning of the third period of Celtic Druids. This phase lasted for about a thousand years, during which the Christian clerics preserved the old stories, myths, and knowledge conveyed by the Druids, most of which converted to Christianity. Thus, the Druid laws, social structure, and ethics were preserved.

The final phase of Celtic Druidism began in the 16th century when European scholars rediscovered the cultural heritage of Druids. The classical Druid texts were translated and printed, which led to the discovery of the sophisticated culture and mannerisms of Druids and Celts, contrary to what people were made to believe about their heritage. This period was considered to be the beginning of the Druid revival, where many groups and societies were established for the sole purpose of rediscovering this concept. Cultural festivals, traditions, and rituals sprang all across Europe, and this revival evolved into a renaissance that continues even today.

Classes of Druids

There was a hierarchical system within the class of Celtic Druids, and they were classified based on their rank and profession. Each class of Druids had a specific color associated with their rank, which also symbolized their role in the Druid system. The eldest and wisest Druids had gold-colored robes. They were also known as the Arch-Druids and were approached when a decision was to be made. Ordinary or general Druids wore white robes and usually acted as priests or teachers. Warrior Druids would wear red robes and were also known as sacrifices. Whereas blue robes were worn by artistic Druids, who were classified as bards. Recruits, although not very common within the Druid culture, were deemed less important than all other classes of Druids and would wear brown or black robes.

All of these subclasses were properly structured and formed a complete hierarchy. Even their life patterns followed the natural cycle. The lunar, solar, and seasonal cycles were strictly observed, and events and rituals were held accordingly.

The End of Ancient Druidism

When Christianity emerged and gradually spread throughout Europe, Druidism's concepts and cultural features faded. Although most Druids converted to Christianity, there were still many Druids in Ireland and nearby Celtic regions, though their number was reduced. Although Druidism was revived and is now heavily practiced, it has since evolved into a much different version of itself. Today, Druids are considered spell casters and mystical arts practitioners.

Chapter 2: Ancient vs. Modern Druidism

Like other Celtic-related religious and cultural organizations, Druidism has survived the test of time and is still being practiced today. However, as you'll see from the comprehensive analysis of the past and present in this chapter, modern Druids have very little in common with their ancestors. Followers of this practice in ancient times were barred from documenting their beliefs and practices. The only evidence we have comes from somewhat questionable Roman sources. The beliefs were passed on to new Druids, who were again prohibited from discussing them with outsiders, especially those representing oppressing religions. The only other sources are the folk tales, which frequently contain other elements of Celtic lore. Therefore, the revival of Druidism is only loosely based on the ancient traditions, as is often pointed out by Celtic reconstructionists. However, despite having no real ties to the ancient practices, the self-proclaimed Druids of modern times continue to thrive.

Druidism represented a closed and somewhat secretive community based on Celtic beliefs.
https://pixabay.com/photos/druid-statue-croome-thinker-1415032/

The Differences and Similarities between the Ancient and Modern Druids

After the 7th century, Druidism was replaced with Christianity and was reduced to a handful of practitioners who were forced to act in utmost secrecy. There were very few sources that would reveal anything about the ancient practices. And until certain groups in Britain and the USA became interested in Druidism in the 18th century, there wasn't much interest in exploring the sources either.

Due to a lack of evidence of how the ancient Druids practiced their art, it's hard to tell just how much modern practices differ. According to Celtic reconstructionist sources, there are quite a few differences between modern Druidism and the ancient Celtic traditions on which ancient Druidism was believed to be based. Yet, these same sources also reveal some similarities between the past and present. To understand this, it first must be noted that most orders of Neo-Druidism claim their origins to be ancient Druid orders of Indo-European. In the West, more traditional Celtic customs were preserved. While in the East, several new Druidic traditions, beliefs, and rituals were born.

The main difference between the old and new traditions is how they are viewed generally. According to ancient lore, in the past, Druidism represented a closed and somewhat secretive community based on Celtic beliefs. Only a few chosen people were initiated into their orders. These were typically the most educated and spiritually gifted ones within the Celtic communities. They conducted ceremonies and enacted spells for special occasions, but pretty much in the same fashion. Neo-Druidism is based on a similar philosophy and way of life for the adherents, except they incorporate different purposes. Instead of self-preservation (which was much needed in ancient times), they now seek a creative awakening of the spirit and are willing to spread it to the younger generations as well. Rather than keeping their nature and polytheistic worshiping practice secret, modern Druids are taking a different approach. This includes incorporating science, art, and holistic techniques to show the benefits of their beliefs.

The Concept of Deity and Sacred Connection

Ancient Druids were polytheists, worshippers of the deities of the Celtic pantheon. Their Neo-Druidic counterparts have kept their practice, but there are also examples of monotheistic or duo-theistic concepts among the practitioners. While the ancestors often revered only one or two deities on special occasions, they never failed to address the others at other times - simply because they feared angering them. In modern times, Druids believe that everyone has a right to honor any number of divine forces and will not be punished for their beliefs.

Pantheism is also a familiar ideology among Neo-Druids, as a supreme god is believed to exist within all beings. A similar, universal life force was also mentioned by the ancestors, although in a somewhat different way. According to them, the life force was given to all beings by the deities. However, the gods and goddesses didn't inhabit the beings. Yet, it allowed the practitioners to stay connected to the natural world, just as it does in modern times. Nature was and is the ultimate source of sacred energy, giving life to animals, humans, and plants alike. Animal guides also received veneration. As people began to consider the ecological benefits of staying close to nature, the concept of animals providing spiritual gifts became more and more acceptable. Whereas animals in the majority of ancient times were only considered tools for rituals, sacrifices, and offerings, now the focus has been shifted to benefiting from them in life. Many animals are respected for their wisdom, healing powers, and vitality.

Reincarnation and Concept of the Otherworld

Reincarnation is another popular concept in Neo-Druidism. Modern Druids believe that souls live successive lives in different forms (animal, human, and inanimate like trees, rocks, etc.). This concept also appears in the sources describing their ancient practices. However, while the ancestors only revered the souls that have passed and asked for their guidance, modern practitioners often try to encourage the souls to move on to the next life through prayers and rituals. Both cultures agree that when a soul leaves its physical body, they rest in the Otherworld. They also agree that this world is only one of the other realms beyond our physical world. Souls can travel between the realms, especially when the barriers between the worlds become thinner, which happens around the solstices. Souls sometimes remain in the Otherworld to either help out the living or because they aren't able to move on. Both ancient and modern Druidic traditions incorporate techniques to communicate with the spirits inhabiting the Otherworld. The most common methods were hypnosis, dream journeying, meditations, and shamanic trances.

Prayers and Rituals

Much like any other spiritual concept, prayer is a fundamental part of a Druid's life. Whether it was assistance from a deity, the protection of their community, a good harvest, or anything else they wanted, ancient practitioners spent days in sacred prayers to obtain it. Nowadays, prayers are more geared towards assistance in spiritual matters. In fact, Neo-Druids are encouraged to use prayers that resonate with them or that they find practical in any situation. Modern Druidic rituals have similar purposes. The ceremonies can deepen one's understanding of purpose and life itself by taking inspiration from ancient Celtic lore and nature. While these rites are somewhat different from the harvest offerings and animal sacrifices presented by their ancestors, they're still performed within sacred stone circles. Even if there aren't any stones surrounding them, the practitioners still celebrate standing in a circle, as this symbolizes their unity. Adherents are often blessed with water, smoke, or by stepping over the fire. They also partake in meditation, which helps them relax, brings inspiration, and allows them to focus on the task ahead. They may not spend days deepening their awareness like their ancestors. Yet, they still take time to do grounding exercises to honor the physical world and the worlds beyond it.

Tolerance and Diversity

As mentioned before, Neo-Druidism encompasses a wide range of beliefs and practices. They don't have any sacred dogma to follow, which allows the adherents to follow their own spiritual path. Those who find it necessary to have a place for worship will choose the groves, places similar both in look and function to churches. They may also seek natural sites surrounded by elements like stones or trees. This practice is equivalent to the ancient Druidic traditions of honoring deities in uninhabited tree groves. Modern Druids may also organize spiritual gatherings with people with different beliefs and religions, showing openness to everyone's points of view on religion, culture, and nature.

The Revival of Druidism

The revival of Druidism is the result of the rise of the rebellious counterculture during the 1960s. In a revolutionary turn of events, people started to realize the need and the benefits of reconnecting with nature. And just like with many other Celtic and pagan regions, the rise of Druidism resulted from the protests against the Christian church. In the USA, a group of students who had mandatory Sunday chapel attendance swapped to a gathering of their newly formed order called The Reformed Druids of North America. At the same time, in Europe, several Druid orders were established, including The Order of Bards Ovates & Druids, founded by historian Ross Nichols. While initially small, these groups have grown Druidism into one of the most well-known spiritual practices.

Before these events, the Druidic traditions were confined to a small group of English and Welsh Druids. And neither of these focused on spirituality as much as the new orders. There are, however, a few honorable mentions, including the efforts of George Watson MacGregor Reid, made at the beginning of the 20th century through The Universal Bond, the religious group Reid led. This group was famous for holding their rituals at Stonehenge and laying the foundation for a more open religion. In fact, it was their efforts that attracted Ross Nichols to Druidism a couple of decades later. Ross was also inspired by other Celtic practices, including Wicca, and adopted a unique cycle of observances. Wanting to work with Druidism differently, he formed what became the world's largest Druid order.

While the group in the USA was formed to free students of an obligation, it still managed to take its hold on the nation. The students who claimed their rights to separate religious acts found what they needed in Druidism. Besides being an alternative option (o which they had no access earlier), Druidism also offered a new way of thinking, something many young people felt the need for. The open-minded philosophies were the perfect addition to the rising counterculture and have developed into rich contemporary practices. Their traditions were recorded so that they could be preserved for future generations. Eventually, these practices have become part of ADF, the largest Druid group in North America today.

Amidst a generation that grew attracted to new beliefs, stories about Druidism and their sacred yet mystical sites like Stonehenge were soon all over the world. Even though little was known about the ancient Druidic heritage of Stonehenge, its mysterious background and the lore around it were enough to pique people's curiosity. It became a popular attraction to those seeking a spiritual journey. John Michell's book, "A View over Atlantis," provided an exceedingly broad insight into nature's spiritual heritage, which spoke to people's spiritual needs.

However, despite all this interest, Druidism as a spiritual practice as we know it today was still only practiced by a few people within each order. This only changed in the 1980s, when the next generation became liberated enough to join Druidism. After this, the number of practitioners quickly grew into the thousands. Around the same time, interest in other alternative beliefs has also started growing. One of these was the New Age movement, which emphasized alternative approaches to spirituality and healing the mind, body, and soul. Celtic spirituality has also become increasingly popular, which is not the case for its modern versions like Wicca or Neo-Paganism. Old manuscripts were examined, and what was left of the ancient ways was rediscovered. Perhaps due to its secretive nature, the tradition of Druidism was one of the most well-researched approaches to the ancient Celtic culture. Even though much of it was based on mythology, it still fueled interest and further research in the following decades.

One of the reasons Druidism became popular in the 1980s is polytheism. People found monotheistic religion too constricting. They needed something that aided their spiritual growth instead of making them seek resolution from one single deity. In fact, many who became interested in Druidism at that time thought that monotheistic religions suppressed spiritual growth so much that it led to crime and other disruptive behavior. Coupled with the world's newfound awareness of the environment and what the technological revolution was doing to the planet, the need for change was never greater. Even though the new traditions were merely based on lore and fiction, people started to believe that to save the planet, they must honor nature. And Druidism, along with other Celtic and pagan traditions, presented the perfect background for this.

Another reason the revival of Druidism was so successful is that instead of presenting itself as a religion with strict rules and expectations, it offered recourse for a spiritual journey. This allowed for a mental exploration that many found much more beneficial than any other religious belief. While the ancient Celtic traditions and philosophy may have inspired this path, it was so accommodating that it seemed to answer many people's needs. By 2000, the number of Druids went over six thousand and was more popular than ever. However, it must be said that despite all the modern influences, the revival of Druidism wasn't just aided by the new cultural movements. The people's newfound awareness of their needs wasn't enough of a driving force to sustain it. No matter how mysterious it may be, the past also had a pivotal influence on re-launching Druidism into the spotlight. If it weren't for writers who became interested in the Celtic lore surrounding Druidism, it would have never risen to the heights it occupies today.

Popular Neo-Druidic Orders

The previous section discussed why Neo-Druidism has become so popular in the past hundred years. But amidst the surge of all kinds of native beliefs, you may be wondering what attracted people to Druidism. After all, there are plenty of other untraditional, mysterious, and magical nature-centered religions and communities. All these represent a novel way of exploring spirituality. Here are a few reasons Neo-Druidic orders have not only become popular but have also risen in numbers:

- **They Provide Simple Answers:** When most people ask questions about life and nature, they often find the simplest answer the most acceptable. Druidism offers uncomplicated solutions, with or without a scientific background, depending on the audience's requirements.

- **Anti-Materialistic Approach**: Unlike other religious organizations that require mandatory contributions, Druid orders only rely on a self-sustained approach and occasional donations from the members of their community.
- **An Escape from Guilt:** Modern Western nations are often plagued by the guilt caused by historical colonialism conducted by their ancestors. Becoming a Druid offers an opportunity of becoming something other than just the descendent of a merciless nation of colonizers.
- **A Chance to Explore Magic:** There is something in magic that piques people's fantasy while allowing it to resonate within. Druidism is one of the few systems that offer both the fantasy of magic and its spiritual benefits.
- **The Accessibility of Information**: Unlike in ancient times when Druidism was practiced in secret, nowadays, everyone can learn the ins and outs of this practice. You can find plenty of information about it online and tailor the wisdom you find to your needs.
- **A Chance for Individualism**: Druidism protects freedom of belief. Even if they embrace the Druid lifestyle, every individual can choose which part of the religion they follow, and they can even change this as they see fit.

Keeping all these benefits and potentially advantageous aspects in mind, there is no wonder that there are significant differences between the various orders. Below are a couple of Druid orders, what they stand for in modern times, and how they differ from ancient beliefs. Before those listed below, we'll mention some of the orders operated before the dawn of the 20th century.

Ancient Order of Druids

The Ancient Order of Druids, or AOD, was established in 1781 in London by Henry Hurle. It was very similar to the Masonic practices, and its adherents were organized by local groups called Lodges. They used very few resources regarding the ancient Druid beliefs and traditions. In fact, they embraced a different approach. They barred discussion of religion and sometimes even philosophy. Instead, they were concerned about the issues of their elitist society.

United Ancient Order of Druids

Growing discontent with the elitist approach, over a hundred original AOD members split – deciding to create a new order called the United Ancient Order of Druids. This order explored the ancient beliefs in great detail, bringing people closer to nature-based traditions. They established new Lodges in rural settings and organized communal programs, which helped people make themselves safer and allowed many to discover new spiritual paths that resonated with them. Over time, this order spread beyond the UK borders and even Europe. After a while, it was renamed the International Grand Lodge of Druidism, one of the most widespread orders in the world.

The Order of Bards, Ovates, and Druids

Founded in 1964, The Order of Bards, Ovates, and Druids is another incredibly influential group of Druidic practitioners. Dividing their practices into three different approaches, they have created a broad range of flourishing communities all over the world. The first of these approaches takes into consideration magic and its connection to nature. The second approach is based on a philosophical approach to spirituality, allowing adherents to express their spirituality through creativity. The third approach concentrates on Shamanism, which creates a dynamic combination of the previous two ideas and unique spiritual beliefs. While still nature-based, these beliefs differ greatly from the ancient Celtic traditions from which Druidism stems.

This order also has set a purpose of further developing modern Druidism, wanting it to become even more accessible to people with different backgrounds and spiritual and cultural beliefs. They also want to incorporate more ancient traditions, including people's reverence towards the land, the sky, the water, and all things natural. While their claims of possessing the original Druidic teachings and originating from the 1970s are often questioned, this order was and continues to be one of the most accommodating and authentic Druid organizations.

The British Druid Order

Also known as BDO, The British Druid Order is another all-encompassing approach to 21-century Druidism. Their teachings are based on Shamanism, environmentalism, positive affirmations, and spiritual awakening. In short, they offer everything spiritual seekers in modern times are looking for. The order was established in 1974 – after a group of highly spiritual people grew highly inspired by a book called

"The White Goddess" (written by Robert Graves) and the works of Mircea Eliade. This order had a unique idea to try to engage with other communities from its early days. In most cases, they only got a response from pagan and occult practitioners. However, this was still very different from the other orders that started out with only a few people studying Druidism without wanting to explore its roots in different Celtic and pagan communities.

The Council of British Druid Orders

Established in 1989, the Council of British Druid Orders encompassed a variety of Druid organizations with different backgrounds and philosophies. While many of the council's founding members have since left the order, the most influential ones still remain. Unlike many other Druid orders, this one places emphasis on keeping up with ancient traditions, especially the reverence toward the sun. They work around this celestial body, honoring its ability to bring nature to life and provide sustenance. They celebrate Solar Festivals with as many members of their community as they can at a time, inviting the different orders to all the major ceremonies. The council's approach is based on a spirit of openness and equality, resonating with the different groups regarding their beliefs, background, or traditions. In this spirit, they've also started a spectacle called Public Ritual, which celebrates the rebirth of the ancient Celtic religion.

Chapter 3: Druidry Basics I: Beliefs, Worlds, and Treasures

The more you learn about the Druids and their fascinating history, the more you wonder about their past and present lives. What were the ancient Druid principles? How did they view the world? What do the modern Druids believe in now? The ancient Druids didn't have the science or information the world has now. They created their beliefs and theories using various mythology and legends that served as the foundation of this belief. In this chapter, you'll take a trip back in history to discover the world of the Druids.

Druidism is a belief that centers around the spiritual nature of life.
https://pixabay.com/photos/pagan-ritual-spiritual-ancient-3892831/

The Druidic Beliefs

Druidism's main focus is spirituality. Some consider it a religion, while others treat it as a way to live their day-to-day lives. At its core, it is a belief that centers around the spiritual nature of life. However, the way they approach this belief differs. Druids are either monotheists, duo-theistic, polytheists, pantheists, or animists. That said, some Druids steer away from all these beliefs and instead believe that the human mind can never know or understand the concept of a Deity.

The monotheistic Druids believe in the existence of one deity. This deity is recognized as a god or a goddess. However, sometimes the gender identity is dismissed altogether, and their deity is just a being that is neither a male nor a female, and they refer to it as the Great Spirit. The duo-theists Druids believe in the existence of two gods. In other words, their deities are a pair of beings, one is female, a Goddess, and one is male, a God. Then you have the polytheistic Druids, who believe in the existence of multiple deities, gods, and goddesses alike. On the other hand, some Druids don't believe in the existence of any deity like the pantheists and the animists. They believe that God exists in everything around them and that everything is God.

This diversity shows how accepting and tolerant Druids are of other people's beliefs. Whether a person worships one god or more - or they don't believe in any god - they can easily find a place in the Druids' religion without any judgments. The truth isn't something fixed, and no one can know for a fact which belief is right or if all of them are wrong. The ancient and new Druids know and accept that not everyone will have the same religious or spiritual beliefs. Up to this day, Druids are still very welcoming and accepting of people and their differences. In fact, diversity has always been one of the main draws to Druidism.

Although all the Druids may not agree on a deity, there is one thing that they all respect and wholeheartedly believe is sacred - nature. They believe that all creatures in nature are equal and that there isn't a being who is more supreme over the other. Humankind merely plays a role in the larger scheme of things, and it certainly isn't the main one.

The Druids hold nature in very high regard, and they find that it nourishes their souls. However, they also believe in the existence of another world, or as they call it, the Otherworld. The Otherworld is a realm that exists beyond the physical world. It's a land of the dead, a place where the spirits go after the body dies. However, the living can also access this place, but they must be unconscious, like during a dream, a shamanic trance, meditation, or when under hypnosis.

Druids are firm believers in the process of reincarnation, which is the soul's rebirth in various physical forms, whether human or not. The Druids and Celts alike believed that one is reborn in the Otherworld when one dies in the physical world. This belief was clear in their funerals which focused on the idea of rebirth rather than treating death as a sad occasion or the end of a person's life cycle.

The Druidic Principles

Druidism is more than just a religion or belief; it is a way of life. The Druids live their lives by a set of principles that serve as the foundation of their teachings.

Love

Love is one of the main principles of Druidism, and it has a broader meaning than just loving all mankind. Since the Druids highly revere nature, they love everything it has to offer, like the animals, the Earth, the stars, and the land. Their love for nature has made them lovers of peace, as they prefer to lead a peaceful existence over one that encourages wars and battles. The ancient Druids were also peace-makers, spreading peace and love wherever they went, which is something the modern Druids still follow. Their love for peace is apparent in their ceremonies as they usually begin them by offering peace. Their love also extends to beauty, not in its superficial meaning but in the beauty of nature and everything it represents. They believe that this beauty serves as an inspiration for artists and poets.

The Druids are fair individuals and encourage justice since it's believed that many of the ancient Druids were lawmakers and judges. The modern Druids were inspired by their ancestors and thus developed a love for justice. Similar to many ancient cultures, they were passionate about the art of story-telling and legends. They believed that stories weren't just meant to entertain but also to bring enlightenment and healing power. The Druids never forgot about their fellow human beings by encouraging deep and meaningful relationships.

Creativity

Creativity plays a huge role in Druidism. Bards, which is a word used to describe poets and storytellers, have always been believers and practitioners of Druidism. During ancient times, the bards wrote stories and songs to help pass on the wisdom of the Druids. Bards also had an impressive and unique memory which enabled them to memorize stories about different lands and tribes. The Celts' love and fascination with the Otherworld were obvious in their creative works. Whether it was music or art, they made the Otherworld a part of their stories, enabling them to create fascinating plots and events. They created tales that showed the world from a different perspective as a place of sensual beauty where creative individuals like artists and craftspeople were respected and honored.

Creativity still remains one of the biggest draws to Druidism. Poets, writers, artists, and any type of creative individuals find that the spirituality Druidism represents can help them foster their creativity, unlike beliefs that center on the importance of the afterlife since it is everlasting while this world will one day wither. Druidism also stresses that life in this realm should be fully lived and experienced. Therefore, people should freely express themselves and share their creativity with the world without hesitation or fear.

Wisdom

As mentioned, the Druids believed in the power of story-telling and used it to pass on their wisdom to their followers. Two of their most famous stories were the story of Taliesin, which took place in Wales, and the story of Fionn mac Cumhaill, which took place in Ireland. Although these stories are very entertaining and full of intriguing events and plot lines, they also contain instructions, symbolism, lessons, and an interesting sequence of events to teach people how to achieve wisdom. These stories were so powerful and inspiring that they became a huge part of Druidism teachings.

Awareness

Awareness is close to the concept of being mindful, which many people incorporate into their daily lives. This concept revolves around the idea that one should be present in the moment and only focus on the here and now. In order to acquire awareness or any skill, one must have high energy levels. For this reason, Druids are always on the lookout for opportunities that can help boost their energy so they can foster their awareness. As one reaches outer and inner awareness, one begins a journey of self-knowledge. When you know who you are and what you are capable of, you are able to make conscious decisions that will benefit your well-being and improve your life.

The Four Sacred Treasures of Tuatha Dé Danann

The Tuatha Dé Danann was a race of supernatural beings that were mentioned in Irish mythology. When they left the heavens and came down to Earth thousands of years ago, they brought with them four sacred treasures. These treasures came from four magical cities, Falis, Gorias, Findias, and Murias, and represent Gaelic sacred principles.

1. The Sword of Nuada

King Nuada of the Tuatha Dé Danann and the god of hunting brought this sword to Ireland from Goris. The sword is a symbol of truth, justice, and the law. According to legend, once this sword is pointed at someone, they will be unable to escape, and when the wielder of the sword asks them a question, they must answer honestly. The sword of Nuada is also called the sword of light, as it was believed that it could bring enlightenment and knowledge.

2. The Spear of Lugh

The spear of Lugh came to earth from the land of Findias. It was an invincible weapon belonging to Lugh of the Long Arm, the ruler of Tuatha Dé Danann and the Celtic god of the sun. This weapon was also referred to as the spear of victory. It was associated with fire and shared some similarities with the sword of Nuada. Both weapons always hit their target. According to legend, the spear was always hot, and the more one used it, the hotter it got. This was extremely dangerous because if the spear reached a certain temperature, it could cause a huge fire that would burn the earth's surface. This is why, every night, the spear was stored in a vessel of water to prevent it from catching fire.

3. The Stone of Destiny

The stone of destiny, which is now referred to as the stone of scone, came to Earth from Falias. According to a legend, a patriarch by the name of Jacob used this stone as a pillow. One day, as he was resting at Bethel in Israel, he saw a vision of angels. This stone had quite a trip before it finally reached Ireland. It was first in Israel and then moved to Egypt, Sicily, then

Spain. In 700 BC, it reached its new home in Ireland. The stone was placed on the hill of Tara, where the kings of Ireland were crowned in the past. Legend says that it would roar when a rightful monarch stood on this stone. England, Ireland, and Scotland used this rock during their royal coronations for centuries.

4. The Cauldron of the Dagda

Dagda was a god, king, and Druid in Irish mythology. The cauldron of the Dagda wasn't an ordinary vessel. It was enchanted since it was bottomless, was always full of food and drinks, and never ran dry. This vessel helped provide for those less fortunate by supplying them with sustenance that never ran out. However, this wasn't the vessel's only "superpower." It could also bring dead soldiers back to life. As a result, the cauldron of the Dagda represented regeneration and rebirth. The cauldron was made in Maurias and was associated with the god Dagda, a great deity and often regarded as a father figure.

Druidic Values

The Druids put a lot of emphasis on character values. Writers who studied ancient and modern Druids narrowed down certain prominent values in this religion.

Responsibility

How a person responds to any situation says a lot about them. Responsibility realizes that every decision you make doesn't only affect you but also impacts all other beings, including future generations. A responsible individual is someone whose actions match their words, keep their promises, and holds themselves accountable when they make mistakes.

Integrity

Integrity is shown in the way a person acts and carries themselves. It's when they are true to themselves and lead authentic lives. These individuals are honest and trustworthy, which is usually clear in their actions and words.

Respect

Respect is treating everyone the same way, usually by showing them understanding and kindness. This value is shown in the diversity of the Druids' beliefs, where they show tolerance by accepting everyone no matter what they believe in. Modern Druids echo the same sentiments by honoring people's differences, whether in their beliefs or lifestyle, by showing others love, compassion, and empathy. Respect is also standing up for what is right and protecting the weak.

Courage

Courage is feeling fear *yet not letting it overpower you;* you still do what's required of you. A courageous person understands the risks of what they are getting themselves into, yet they do it if it will benefit others. These are usually the people who can change the world as they do the right thing, even if hardships and suffering await them on the other side.

Druidic Theories on Cosmology

Unlike other ancient cultures that believed the universe was unstable and could break down at any minute, the Druids believed that neither the world nor the human soul was destructible. That said, they believed that fire and water have the power to wreak havoc. According to ancient Irish texts, the fire would cause the apocalypse and end the world. Irish and Scottish folklore predict the end of the world when the heavens collapse over the earth and the earth crashes into the ocean.

There are various myths of creation about how the world came to be in Celtic mythology. One legend tells the story of a god and goddess who went by the names Donn and Danu. These two deities came into existence from the great void. They fell in love with each other from the moment their eyes met, and this love produced several children. Another myth states that it was giants, not gods, who created the earth. One powerful giant was melted by fire, and his remains formed the world. The oceans, seas, and rivers were born from his blood, his hair made the forests, his skull became the sky, and his bones formed the mountains.

The Druidic Branches

There are three branches of ancient Druidism, the bard, the ovate, and the Druids. The bards were poets, singers, and storytellers. They were also satirists who criticized and sometimes praised powerful figures and war heroes. Bards used the power of the word to act as cheerleaders to soldiers and satirized those who deserved it. Their talent was so powerful that it seemed that they had a superpower strong enough to overthrow kings.

The second branch is the ovate, the natural philosophers. The ovaries, also referred to as the *ovates*, played a big role in ancient Celtic religion, and their main focus was divination. They predicted the future by killing living creatures and watching them die, and then observing their remains. For this reason, they were considered priests of death. However, they weren't allowed to make these sacrifices alone as a Druid must be present, which is why it was believed that the Druids were the real priests of death. The ovates might have only served as executioners. However, there could be confusion about the role both ovates and Druids played in these sacrifices, as the Druids might not have outranked them. However, their exact role in the sacrifices remains a mystery as so much about the Druids has failed to reach us.

The last branch is the Druids. The Druids were the highest rank above both the bards and the ovates. They answered no one, and the kings' Druids were treated with the utmost respect. The king's Druid was the only one who was allowed to speak before the king. The Druids were involved in the biggest decisions in the court of the kings, for example, deciding whether the king should go to battle or not.

The Land, Sky, and the Sea

You probably know the four elements as air, water, fire, and earth. However, the Druids had a different interpretation that involved only three elements, the land, the sky, and the sea. These elements are referred to as the Celtic elements. The sea represented water, the land represented earth, and the sky represented the air and fire. The three elements can also represent different realms. The sky is the Upperworld, the land is the Middleworld, and the sea is the Underworld. The Druids used these three realms in many of their rituals. These realms were very powerful, and the Celtic took them very seriously. This was obvious in an ancient oath that they took when they made a promise. It usually goes something like this "If I break my promise, may the sky fall down on me, may the earth open up and devour me, and may the sea drown me." The Druids also used these elements in their prayers and folk magic.

The Celts believed that these three elements or realms made the whole world. The fairies lived in the Underworld or the sea. The land, or the Middleworld, was the physical realm where all living and non-living things existed, like humans, animals, stones, trees, and plants. Trees and stones were highly revered because they existed in between realms. Trees existed between the three realms, with their roots in the Underworld, trunks in the Middleworld, and branches in the Upper world. The stones could exist between two realms, with one half above the ground and the other half under the ground.

The Five Directions

According to ancient Celtic myths, there were twelve significant sacred directions to create a ritual space. Historians gathered this information as there were twelve winds that affected the people and lands in a distinctive way. However, later these twelve directions were reduced to only five. It is believed that religion played a role in their reduction. The five directions were featured in various Celtic stories and legends. Each of these directions had its own emblem and was represented by a creature that was an animal, bird, or fish.

The first direction is the North, represented by an emblem of a sword, and its creature is an eagle. The winds that come from this direction serve as a warning of an impending conflict. This direction is extremely significant since it is the direction of the Gods, battles, and warriors.

The second direction is the East, and it serves as a direction for prosperity and abundance. Salmon is this direction's creature, while its emblem is wealth. This wealth can be represented in anything like fine clothes, honey, or good earth.

The third direction is the South which is considered the Goddess direction. There is something quite enchanting and artistic about this direction since it is associated with water and creative arts like poetry and music. It is represented by the sow. The sow is an animal that hides in the darkest corners of the earth, looking for food and inspiration. It can find hidden treasures in the darkest parts of the earth and bring them to the surface.

The fourth direction is the west and is represented by the stag. This is the direction where imagination can run wild, creating stories of past and present. It is a place for illumination, igniting a fire in one's soul, telling stories, preserving history, and sharing mysteries. The west serves as a home for intellectuals where they can exercise their creativity.

The last direction is the center that completes the ritual space making it a whole. Interestingly, this is the fifth direction, and the number five is associated with a sacred whole. The animal representing this direction is the mare of Sovereignty which represents the Goddess of the land. The emblem associated with the fifth direction is the stone.

Whether it was their beliefs, principles, or values, the Druids have definitely taught the world so much. These non-judgmental individuals have passed down their beliefs to modern Druids making their ceremonies diverse and a place where people can celebrate their differences without judgment or criticism. This diverse environment that modern Druidism fostered has attracted many people to this belief. The history of Druidism doesn't stop here; you have only just scratched the surface. In the next chapter, you'll learn more about the Druids' love and respect for nature and all its beings.

Chapter 4: Druidry Basics II: Nature, Cycles, and Seasons

The Druids have always had a very special relationship with nature. Although they don't worship nature, they consider it sacred and even see god in it. Many druids are animistic, so they see God in everything, including nature. At the same time, others are pantheists and believe that everything has a soul, mainly in nature. That said, what is nature according to the Druids? Most people apply the term nature to trees, mountains, forests, animals, or anything that isn't man-made. However, the Druids' definition of nature is much broader. According to the Druidism belief, nature is everything, and this applies not only to the physical world but to everything beyond this world. The word supernatural doesn't exist in the Druids' dictionary because everything in this realm or the other is within what they believe is nature.

The word Druid is derived from doire, which is an Irish Gaelic word for an oak tree.
https://pixabay.com/photos/root-tree-root-druid-grove-forest-389737/

Whatever belief Druids followed, whether it was animism, pantheism, monotheism, polytheism, or any other belief, they all saw nature as something divine. The Druids didn't have the technology or the science that the world has today to send rockets to space and explore the universe. As a result, they regarded the universe as something mysterious, so powerful that the simple human mind would never be able to fully comprehend it.

Connecting with nature was of the utmost importance to the Druids. Maybe they didn't need to comprehend this immense sacred power, but they still sought to be one with it. The Druids used meditations, rituals, and revering to establish a deep connection with nature. Although most Druids used the same methods to connect with nature, the result was different. This connection was more of a personal experience and differed from one person to the other. It was a feeling deep inside of them that consumed them and made them feel one with the universe. Imagine your spirit reaching out to communicate with the spirit of nature; no words can describe this experience.

There is a misconception among people who aren't familiar with Druidism that Druids worship nature. It is understandable why anyone would think so. With how they revered and treated nature, it may seem that nature is their god. However, the Druids revered nature as an expression of a deity but not as a deity itself.

Nature isn't only revered, but it is also celebrated. In this chapter, you'll learn about sacred Druids' holidays and other nature-related events and creatures that were connected with the Druids and the Celtic culture.

The Wheel of the Year

The wheel of the year in Druidism is a set of eight holidays that usually celebrate the new season, with each holiday taking place every seven weeks. These holidays were an old tradition that existed at the time of the ancient Druids. However, modern Druids revived these festivals to celebrate nature through various rituals every year. These eight holidays create a perfect balance as four of them are solar while the other four are lunar. Many people find that solar holidays are more modern. Thus, they usually associate them with neo-Druidism.

These eight holidays not only celebrate the life cycles of nature, animals, and plants, but they are also a time to honor the Druid's connection with the realms of the animals and plants. These festivals show

how intertwined people's bodies and minds are with nature as these celebrations strengthen their bonds with it. The Druids regard the change in the seasons with gratitude and appreciation rather than something they take for granted. One can learn many lessons when one season ends and another begins.

Samhain (October 31st - November 2nd)

Although the Gregorian calendar celebrates the new year on January 1st, the Celtic new year was on October 31st during the time of Samhain. Does this date look familiar? In fact, Samhain was the origin of Halloween, which many people around the world celebrate each year. Many of its traditions, like trick or treat, were inspired by pagan practices. At this time of the year, the veil between the world of the living and the dead becomes thinner, and the spirits of the dead can travel between the two worlds. The Celts considered Samhain a time to honor their departed ancestors. According to the Druids, there are three types of ancestors, ancestors of the lands, ancestors of spiritual traditions, and ancestors of blood.

The Celts were known for having a highly structured society where everyone had to abide by a certain set of rules. However, these rules didn't apply to Samhain as this was the time when the order took a step back, allowing chaos to reign. People let loose during these few days, similar to Halloween. They would dress up, children would go trick or treating, and people would do the craziest things you can imagine. Samhain is ruled by the goddess of the winter months, Cailleach, who was also called the Gray Hag and the Dark Woman of Knowledge.

There is something extremely genuine yet sad about this holiday because of its close connection to death. It is also the time to prepare for the cold and dark winters.

Winter Solstice (21st December)

The ancient Druids referred to the winter solstice as the Alban Arthan, which means the light of Arthur. The winter solstice is a time for death and rebirth. It marks the beginning of winter and one of the darkest times of the year when the sun disappears for the next few months. Most people associate darkness with fear or sadness. However, the Druids had a different point of view. They didn't see darkness as something evil or scary because it's a natural part of life, just like light. The Druids understood the importance of darkness as it made people appreciate the light even more. Instead of spending the winter months in sadness and counting the days until it's over, the Druids took this time to rest their bodies and allow their lands to rest and regenerate as well.

Imbolc (February 1st)

The ancient Druids called this festival two names, Imbolc and Oimelc. Don't let the date fool you; Imbolc isn't a winter celebration. In fact, the Celts celebrated Imbolc to mark the beginning of spring. It is the first of three spring celebrations that are part of the wheel of the year. The Imbolc is the time of the year that marks the first snowdrop and witnesses the snow melt. During this time, lambs are born, and the world begins to prepare itself to welcome the spring. It is a simple yet beautiful festival where people honor the Mother Goddess by forming a ceremonial circle and lighting eight candles at its center. The Imbolc festival is ruled by Brighid, the goddess of healers and poets.

Spring Equinox (March 21st)

The Spring Equinox is the second spring celebration in the wheel of the year. It is the time of the year when the day is as long as the night. 21st March marks the beginning of spring when the cold months of winter are over, the sun wakes up from its long slumber, and people finally begin witnessing the first signs of spring. As spring finally arrives and the weather gets warmer, people take advantage of this special time to grow plants and make all the plans and projects they put off during the cold and dark weather. Spring Equinox, or Alban Eilir, which means the light of the Earth, is the time of year when the flowers begin blooming, and the plants seem in a hurry to grow and cover the lands.

Beltane (May 1st)

Beltane is the last of the three spring festivals. It marks the time of the year when the lands are fertile again, which is what Beltane celebrates, the fertility of the lands. Beltane was an interesting festival to celebrate, with the Celts taking to the streets to dance and build maypoles and bonfires. They would bless their cattle by riding them through the bonfire smoke to guarantee they would be fertile and healthy for the rest of the year. The cattle most likely enjoy these trips after spending the whole winter in confinement. One of the main Beltane celebrations that usually takes place in Ireland is the lighting of the fires of Tara. It is the first fire the Irish light every year, and they use its flames to light more fires.

Think of the Imbolc as the beginning of your childhood, while the Beltane is the time of adolescence. What you sow in your childhood, you reap in your late childhood. The same applies to the seasons - you reap the seeds you planted during Imbolc in Beltane.

Summer Solstice (June 21st)

Now the sun is shining bright to mark the first days of the summer. The summer solstice or Alban Hefin, which means the light of the shore, is the time to celebrate the arrival of the summer with its heat and fiery sun. This is usually the longest day of the year. The Druids chose this day to hold their most complicated ceremony. These festival celebrations usually begin on its eve at midnight by holding a vigil around the fire all night. As the sun shines to mark the beginning of a new day, another ceremony takes place. This ceremony, which is referred to as the dawn ceremony, celebrates the sun rising in all its glory on this long and powerful day. Later in the day, another ceremony is held, usually at noon.

Lughnasadh (August 1st)

The Lughnasadh festival celebrates the first harvest since, during this time of year, the grains and vegetables are fully grown, ripe, and ready for harvest. This is a fun festival to celebrate, whether in ancient or modern Druidism, where people play games, gather summer fruits with their loved ones, and plan various festivities. An interesting ceremony usually takes place in some areas during Lughnasadh, where people set a wheel on fire and send it rolling down a hill. This is a symbol of the year's descent as winter approaches. The wheel also holds a deeper meaning in Druidism, as the Druids would hold ceremonies to pass a wheel around a circle to symbolize a year ending and the beginning of the next.

Fall Equinox

The fall/autumn equinox is also called Alban Elfed, which means light of the water, and it is the eighth festival in the wheel of the year. This is the beginning of fall, and similar to the spring equinox, the day is equal to the night. However, this won't last long as the days will become shorter and the nights longer to prepare for the cold winter. The fall equinox is another holiday that celebrates harvesting. During this time, people collect fruits and vegetables to store them for the cold months. The Lughnasadh festival marks the beginning of harvest, while the fall equinox marks the end of the harvesting season. Since this is one of the most balanced days of the year, it encourages people to find balance within themselves, their lives, and their lands. During this festival, people plan ceremonies where they give thanks to the Mother Goddess and to the fruits of the earth.

Trees and Mother Nature

Trees played a big part in Druidism. In fact, the word Druid is derived from doire, which is an Irish Gaelic word for an oak tree. It means "one with knowledge of the oak." Although the Druids considered all trees to be sacred, the oak tree held a significant place in their hearts and was highly revered by the Celts and the Druids alike. The tree represented nobility, strength, wisdom, courage, and truth. The Druids believed that the oak tree possessed knowledge more than any other, and if one could possess its knowledge, one would gain the knowledge of all the other trees. They have a very special relationship with all trees as they become one with them and take in their knowledge.

Some people study more than one branch of Druidism, like those who study to become ovates. One of the main things they focus on is mastering the skill of working with the powers of nature. Students learn the Ogham alphabet and form close bonds with the trees. They treat trees as living creatures with souls and reap all their benefits, like gifts and medicine. They also study herbalism to help them heal different ailments.

Fairy Folk

You are probably familiar with fairies, as they are featured in multiple movies and TV shows. According to fairy lore, these creatures don't live in the physical world but in a world that is invisible to human beings. The fairies had their own king called *Oberon,* and queen Tatiana. The concept of the fairies is very old, as they first came to be in Ireland in the 12th century. Although movies and cartoons portray fairies as cute little creatures who spread fairy dust to spread joy and good luck, fairy lore is different. In fact, fairies are associated with death since, according to legends, the spirit of the dead would travel to the fairies' locations. Some fairies also foretold the death of a person, like banshees, or summoned the spirits of the dead.

According to the ancient Irish, fairies were the first creatures to occupy the country. Not all fairies looked like their portrayal in the media. Some fairy folks were the same size as the average person and often dressed in green attire. They were sometimes portrayed as grotesque creatures or tiny ones that could fly like Tinkerbell or creatures that could turn invisible at will. Since there are hundreds of types of fairies, naturally, they won't all look the same.

These creatures had interesting superpowers, like changing their appearance and disappearing at will. People didn't regard fairies as regular creatures. They considered them to be god-like. Fairies were gifted musicians, and singers would often credit fairies for providing them with talent and inspiration. In the past, people were afraid to call fairies by their name, so they would refer to them as the noble folks, hidden people, the good folks, or the little people.

Some fairies look like regular people, while others are tiny and can fly, so what does that make them? Well, most people had different opinions of what category the fairies fell under. Some consider the fairies to be the spirits of the dead, fallen angels, or ghosts. Either way, they were creatures who weren't all bad or all good, so they didn't belong in Heaven or Hell.

Some fairies would kidnap a child from a household for various reasons. This could be for revenge, to be a servant, or to allow the fairies to love and be loved by a child. When they kidnap someone, they often leave a changeling in their place, which is a fairy that looks exactly like the child or person they kidnapped. The changelings were often wise creatures but very odd. If someone found out about them, they would be forced to return the person they had kidnapped and then disappear.

Some fairies were good and helpful and were considered guardian fairies that would help people around the house. However, these fairies were extremely ugly and even a little terrifying to look at. Another type of fairy that was very popular in Irish folklore is the banshee. A banshee often takes the shape of a woman, either a beautiful woman, pale-skinned and with long red or silver hair, or an old woman dressed in black and covering her face with a veil. These creatures are considered omens of death. If a banshee screams outside a house, then a member of this family is about to die. It is important to note that they don't kill or cause death; they only warn that death is coming for someone.

Many people in Ireland found fairies to be terrifying creatures because they believed that they were responsible for any misfortune that befell them. People would even avoid interfering with them on the night of Samhain/Halloween. To this day, people still believe in fairies, and there are many stories of people insisting that they have encountered one.

Green Spirituality

As the name suggests, green spirituality is a type of spirituality that is concerned with the planet. It should be no surprise that the Druids care about the environment since they highly revere nature and normally want to protect it. In fact, some of their spiritual traditions centered around the environment. Practicing green spirituality allows you to connect with Earth and care about all its creatures. This type of spirituality doesn't revolve around a deity and only focuses on the planet. It is important to note that this isn't a religion; it merely adjusts your perceptions of the planet and all its creatures.

Looking at all the Druids' festivities, it is fairly obvious how they cared about and respected nature. Each holiday in the wheel of the year celebrates nature in one way or another. The Druids' respect for nature was clear in their love and appreciation of the environment. They understand that earth is their home, and they should protect it against harm by being environmentally conscious.

Modern Druids still celebrate the wheel of the year with various activities like cooking a good meal and inviting friends and family over, meditation, building an altar, practicing rituals, harvesting, planting, or dancing. Remember to always give thanks to Mother Nature during these festivities for all the gifts that it has given you, whether it's the heat of the sun after a cold winter or the harvest and the fertility of the land.

There is still more that you should know about the Druids, mainly their myths and legends. You can learn so much about a culture from their stories as they usually reflect their morals and beliefs. The next chapter will dive into all the fascinating tales about the Druids and their gods and battles. So, prepare yourself for a journey that will fire your imagination.

Chapter 5: Druidry Basics III: Myths and Legends

Can you imagine a world without myths and legends? A world without mythical creatures, heroes, brave soldiers, or battles fought with blood, sweat, and tears sounds like a boring world, right? Although myths are make-believe stories, they are usually inspired by a culture's traditions, and some may even have factual origins. There is no denying that legends are entertaining, but they also serve a higher purpose. The stories are sacred and reflect real human experiences that everyone can easily relate to, even today. Every generation can benefit from the tales of their ancient ancestors.

Myths are usually inspired by a culture's traditions, and some have factual origins.
https://pixabay.com/photos/book-read-old-literature-books-1659717/

The myths and legends in Druidism are full of tales about heroism and mythical creatures that are entertaining and can give you an idea of the principles that Druids and Celts believed in back then. These legends have played a significant role in the lives of modern Druids and Celts. Let's go on an adventure to a world of fantasy filled with magic, deities, and supernatural creatures that will spark your imagination.

The Mabinogion

The Mabinogion is an ancient book that consists of eleven mythical Welsh tales. This book has left its mark on British literature, as it contains some of the oldest stories the country has ever known. These tales showcase the Celtic history, traditions, and folklore that took place in a magical fantasy land that is quite similar to Wales. The Mabinogion tells stories of heroes, magic, and dragons that will make you wonder if you are reading an ancient book or Game of Thrones. In fact, Welsh mythology has had a huge impact on modern culture. For instance, people transforming into animals, strange sexual relationships, and the character of Bran Stark from Game of Thrones were all inspired by tales and characters from the Mabinogion book. The Mabinogion also featured the legend of king Arthur, his sword Excalibur, Merlin, and the knights of the round table.

The book was originally titled "Mabinogi," which is derived from the word "mab," which translates to youth or boyhood. However, Lady Charlotte Guest was the first person to translate and publish The Mabinogion; she gave it this name as she thought it was the plural of Mabinogi. Although this book is extremely significant in the literary world and the Druids' culture, the author of these tales remains a mystery. The stories in these books are ancient, and the Celts never wrote anything down, and all their stories were passed down by word of mouth. Therefore, these tales never stuck to their original material, and each person telling these stories would probably add their own spin on them. However, they were written down and finally preserved.

Modern Druids hold The Mabinogion in very high regard. They highly revere some of the fake deities that were featured in this book. They feel connected to these stories as if they spoke to them. The books also echoed ancient traditions that some modern Druids may find inspiring.

The book is divided into three categories:
1. The Four Branches of the Mabinogi
2. The Four Independent/Native Tales
3. The Three Romances

The four branches consist of four stories which are some of the book's most ancient tales. They also feature very mythological themes. The tales don't revolve around one person, but one character, Pryderi, is featured in the four stories. The themes in these stories usually revolve around conflict, shifts in power, and misfortune.

Pwyll

The first story/branch is the tale of Pwyll. This tale took place in the south of Wales. This place shared a deep connection with Annwn, which was believed to be a magical underworld. The story was named after its main character Pwyll. Pwyll was a king who ruled over a magical land called Dyfed. He wanted to be the head of Annwn, so he underwent multiple transformations until he achieved his goal and finally earned the title. He also developed a close friendship with the king of Annwn, Arwan. Pwyll fell in love with a Goddess named Rhiannon, but he wasn't the only one who was after her heart. A man under the name of Gwawl also wanted to marry the goddess. Both men were rivals, and Gwawl used trickery on Pwyll to be able to marry Rhiannon. However, the goddess chose to marry Pwyll instead.

The married couple had a child named Pryderi, whom Gwawl kidnapped right after his birth. However, the baby's nurses accused his own mother, Rhiannon, of killing her child. As a result, Rhiannon was severely punished until the child was discovered and returned to his father. Pryderi succeeded his father as king of Dyfed.

Branwen

The second story/branch is the tale of Branwen. The tale revolves around three main characters Bran the Blessed, who was the giant king of Britain; his sister Branwen whom the story is named after; and Efnisien, who was their evil half-brother. In order to restore the peace between Ireland and Britain, Bran arranged for his sister Branwen to marry Matholwch, the king of Ireland. Efnisien felt disrespected when his brother made this decision without consulting him. He acted out of anger and killed

Matholwch's horses. Bran remedied the situation by giving Matholwch many expensive gifts, including new horses and a magic cauldron that has the power to bring the dead back to life. Matholwch accepted Bran's gesture, and he and Branwen got married and lived in Ireland.

Branwen gave birth to a son whom they named *Gwern*. However, the people of Ireland couldn't accept Branwen as their queen because they never got over Efnisien's actions and the murder of the horses. They demanded their king take action against these heinous acts that insulted the people. Matholwch listened to his people and punished his wife. He banished Branwen to the kitchen in his castle, where she worked daily. However, this wasn't enough for Matholwch. He also had a butcher beat her every day. Branwen couldn't take it anymore and sent a letter to her brother, who had no idea of the suffering his sister was enduring, to come and save her.

When the letter reached Bran, he didn't think twice. He took an army and traveled to Ireland to save his sister right away. Matholwch wanted to make peace with Bran, so he promised Bran that he would abdicate the throne and make Gwern a king instead. Matholwch held a coronation feast. However, it didn't go as planned. Efnisien interfered again when he felt disrespected by his brother's actions. He attacked and killed Irish men during the coronation and killed his nephew Gwern as well. As a result, peace was no longer an option. He hid under the dead bodies to protect himself from the fighting. The Irish decided to use the magic cauldron to revive their dead. They threw all the dead men into the cauldron, including Efnisien, whom they didn't know was there, but he broke into pieces and died.

The Irish lost the battle, and only seven Welsh soldiers survived. Although Bran was one of the survivors, he was mortally wounded. He ordered his soldiers to cut off his head and bury it in London. Branwen left with the remaining Welsh soldiers to Wales, but her heart couldn't handle the grief of losing her son and brother, and she died as well. In Ireland, five pregnant women survived, and their children repopulated the country.

Manawydan

Manawydan is the third branch/story, and it tells the tale of Bran's brother, Manawydan, and one of the seven soldiers that survived the battle in Branwen's tale. Manawydan's story begins right after he buries Bran's head. After his brother's passing, he was the only legitimate heir to the throne. He married Rhiannon after her husband, Pwyll, passed away. However, Dyfed fell under an enchantment that caused everyone to disappear, including animals. Only four people didn't disappear Manawydan, Rhiannon, her son from Pryderi, and his wife, Cigfa. They moved to England, where they made a living by making shields and saddles. Their work was impeccable, which caused jealousy from other craftsmen who plotted to kill them. Pryderi wanted to stay back and fight these men, but they decided it was better to go back to Dyfed.

One day Manawydan and Pryderi went hunting and encountered a while boar. Pryderi followed the boar even though Manawydan warned him against it. He ended up in an empty and mysterious fort and eventually got stuck in a magical cauldron. Rhiannon grew worried about her son and went to look for him. She found the fort and got stuck in the cauldron as well. Afterward, the fort vanished with both the mother and son. Manawydan and Cigfa moved again to England after losing their loved ones. However, they suffered the same fate of encountering jealous rivals and had to return to Dyfed. He and Cigfa began working in farming, but his farm was stripped bare. He then found out that a fat mouse was stealing their corn.

Manawydan caught the mouse, and as he was about to kill it, three men came to him and offered him a ransom to let the mouse go. One of the three men was a bishop whom Manawydan asked to lift the curse off Dyfed and bring back his wife and stepson. It turned out that these three men were Llwyd ap Cil Coed, the person that cast the spell in the first place. He wanted to avenge Gwawl (from the first story) and kidnap Rhiannon and Pryderi. The mouse that Llwyd desperately wanted to free was his wife, who was pregnant with his child. Llwyd lifted the spell, and Dyfed returned to its glory.

Math

Math is the last story/branch in the first category. This is by far the most complicated story of the four branches. This tale revolves around Lleu Llaw Gyffes, a Celtic hero and a Druid god. The story begins with a man named Math, the ruler of Gwynedd and the son of Mathonwy. Math had a nephew named Gilfaethwy who fell in love with a young girl named Goewin, who was Math's foot holder. Math was required to rest his feet in a virgin woman's lap except when in battle, or he would die. Gilfaethwy wanted Goewin for himself, but she was always with his uncle. Gilfaethwy's brother Gwydion, who was a magician, helped his brother distract the king so Goewin would be alone.

Gwydion told Math of a new animal, which was the pig, and the only person who had it was Pryderi, who became the king of Dyfed in this story. Gwydion tricked Pryderi into giving them the pigs, but Pryderi found out, and he waged war against Math. During the battle, Gilfaethwy took advantage of this opportunity and raped Goewin. Math and Pryderi faced each other in single combat, which ended with Math killing Pryderi.

Math went back home, and when he rested his feet in Goewin's lap, he realized that she was no longer a virgin. Math discovered what happened when he was gone, banished his nephews for their actions, and married Goewin to protect her honor. When their punishment was over and they returned, Math asked them to recommend another virgin foot holder. Gwydion told the king that his sister Arianrhod could fulfill the new role. What they didn't know was that Arianrhod wasn't a virgin. She was supposed to prove her virginity to Math, but at this moment, she gave birth to a son. She was shamed and left her son, and ran away. As she was escaping, she dropped a lump of flesh which Gwydion kept to find out later that it was a second child. The first child was named Dylan, who, while he was getting baptized, jumped into the sea and took on the characteristics of a fish. Gwydion grew attached to the second child but didn't give him a name as he wanted Arianrhod to acknowledge and name her son. When the boy turned four, Gwydion took him to his sister, who was ashamed and refused to acknowledge or name him. However, Gwydion tricked his sister into naming the boy who was Lleu Llaw Gyffes.

Lleu Llaw Gyffes grew up to be a strong boy. However, his mother cursed him so that he was never able to fight until she bestowed this gift on him. Gwydion decided to trick his sister again to help Lleu, but she figured it out and cursed Lleu to never have a human wife. Math and Gwydion made a woman from flowers taken from the oak tree and named her Blodeuwedd to be Lleu's wife.

One day, Blodeuwedd met a nobleman, and they both fell in love with each other. The lovers decided to kill Lleu so that they could be together. They tricked Lleu and stabbed him with a spear, but he was only wounded. Lleu turned into an eagle and fled. Gwydion and Math found Lleu and helped him until his wounds healed. Lleu was adamant about finding his wife and her lover to get his revenge. Blodeuwedd was terrified, so she decided to escape. However, Gwydion found her and cursed her into an owl. Blodeuwedd's lover, named Gronw, offered Lleu money so he wouldn't exact vengeance. However, Lleu told him that he would only accept his offer if he threw a spear at him, just like Gronw did to him. Gronw agreed, but the spear went right through him, and he died. Lleu then succeeded his uncle as king.

Tuatha de Dannan and the Fomorians

The tale of Tuatha de Danann and the Fomorians belongs to Irish mythology and is one of the most significant tales in Celtic and Druid history. The Tuatha de Dannan was a very powerful supernatural race of divine beings. The Tuatha de Danann translates to "the followers of Danu," the mother Goddess who was worshiped by The Tuatha de Danann. When they arrived in Ireland, the Tuatha de Dannan bestowed their wisdom upon the people of Ireland and taught them various skills. They also brought four treasures to Ireland that were mentioned in a previous chapter.

These divine beings resembled human beings. They were tall, with green or blue eyes and blonde or red hair. According to legend, these beings were very beautiful and highly revered for their powers. No one knows for a fact how the Tuatha de Dannan arrived in Ireland. Sources vary on the method they used to land; some say that they flew, while others believe they landed in Ireland on a dark cloud.

The Fomorians were another race of supernatural beings and were some of the early settlers in Ireland. The Fomorians were the opposite of the Tuatha de Dannan in everything. For starters, they were ugly giants who looked like monsters with dark skin and dark hair. They were described as having one eye, one arm, and one leg. Some accounts described them as having human-like bodies with goat heads.

Scholars can't agree on what the name Fomorians mean. They know that "Fo" means "beneath." Some believe that the second part of their name, "mor," means sea, while others believe it means "spirit." This can mean that these supernatural beings either came from the sea or the underworld. Similar to the Tuatha de Danann, no one knows exactly how the Fomorians arrived in Ireland. However, some believe that they got there by ship.

The Tuatha de Dannan was at war with another race of people called Firbolgs, who were the rulers of Ireland before the Tuatha de Dannan.

Both races agreed to split the country between them, with the Tuatha de Dannan taking the bigger part. Before making peace, the battle between the two races was fierce, and Nuada, the king of Tuatha de Dannan, lost his arm. This prevented Nuada from being king because, according to their laws, one must be in perfect shape to be a king. Nuada had no choice but to abdicate the throne. However, it was temporary because, seven years later, the king would get an iron hand and reclaim his throne.

During these seven years, Bres was the king of Tuatha de Danann. Bres' mother was from the Tuatha de Dannan, while his father was a Fomorian. Unlike Nuada, whom his people loved, Bres was extremely unpopular as he favored the Fomorians over the Tuatha de Danann. When the seven years were over, and Nuada was ready to reclaim his throne, Bres was bitter. He joined the Fomorians and waged war against the Tuatha de Danann. Refugees from the Firbolg supported this war as it provided them with an opportunity to exact vengeance on the Tuatha de Danann. The king of the Fomorians, Balor, killed Nuada. The Tuatha de Danann champion was a man named Lugh Lamhfada. He was also half-Fomorian and Balor's grandson. Unlike Bres, he was loyal to the Tuatha de Danann and killed his grandfather to avenge Nuada. Lugh became the king of the Tuatha de Dannan and established peace between the two races. He was a just king and ruled over the people for forty years.

The Legend of Cuchulainn

Cuchulainn was the son of Lugh (the god of the sun), and his legend belonged to Irish-Celtic mythology. Cuchulainn's original name was Setanta, but he acquired his new name later in life. There was a man called Culann the Smith, whom the king of Ulster and his guards were feasting within his house. Setanta wanted to reach the king's court, but Culann's guarding hound prevented him from getting in, so Setanta killed it. Culann's heart broke when he lost his hound, so Setanta offered to be Culann's guard instead, and he became to be known as Cuchulainn, which means "the hound of Culann." Cuchulainn was a great warrior, and he went to Ireland to become Ulster's champion. Ulster was going to war against Connacht and its queen, Medb. During the battle, Cuchulainn found himself coming face to face with his childhood best friend, Ferdia, whom Cuchulainn ended up killing. When Cuchulainn was in battle, he became so consumed with fighting that he was not able to recognize whom he was fighting or even tell the difference between a friend and an enemy.

The beautiful princess Emer came into Cuchulainn's life, and they got married. However, their happiness didn't last as Cuchulainn fell in love with a fairy princess named Fand. When Emer found out, she was understandably jealous. However, the jealousy didn't last as Fand returned to her husband. There were multiple people whose feelings got hurt, so Manannan, the king of the Otherworld, cast a spell to make all parties involved forget. Queen Medb tricked Cuchulainn and lured him, and left him for her soldiers to kill him. According to legend, his death was foretold, and the goddess Maorriagn transformed into a crow and stood over his shoulder in his final moments.

The Four Cycles of Mythological Sagas and Legends

Irish mythology is divided into four cycles to help you better understand the timeline of these tales.

The Mythological Cycle

The mythological cycle is the oldest cycle in Irish mythology. Myths in this cycle include tales about divine beings who were some of the early settlers in Ireland, like the Tuatha de Dannan. When Christianity arrived in Ireland, the Tuatha de Dannan came to be referred to as Aos Sí or the fairy folk. The Tuatha de Dannan settled in Ireland before humans occupied it. After the Tuatha de Danann, another race occupied Ireland, and it was called Milesians. Since the stories in this cycle involve supernatural creatures, there is little or no logic in the series of events. For instance, in one story, a character turned into a fly, but a noblewoman swallowed her and then got pregnant and gave birth to a baby girl. The baby girl was the woman who turned into a fly.

When the rule of the Tuatha de Danann ended, they still appeared in stories from the other cycles. It is important to note that neither the Tuatha de Dannan nor any characters in this cycle were considered gods. They just had god-like qualities and appearances.

The Ulster Cycle

The second cycle contains some of the most popular stories in Irish lore that took place in the first century. The Ulster cycle is different from the mythological cycle in its portrayal of Ireland; it was no longer a united country ruled by a king. The country was divided into regions, each having its own ruler. Most of the tales in this cycle revolve around the battles fought between the different regions. This cycle includes the tale of Cú Chulainn and the tragedy of Deirdre.

The Fenian Cycle

All tales in this cycle revolve around members of Fianna and Fionn Mac Cumhaill. This cycle began right after the Ulster cycle and before the cycle of the kings. It doesn't deal with supernatural beings or kings but deals with hunters and heroes. The events in this cycle took place between the 7th and 14th centuries. Some of the legends featured in this cycle include The Boyhood Deeds of Fionn and Salmon Knowledge.

The Cycle of Kings/Historian Cycle

This is the last cycle in Irish mythology and includes tales about the Gaelic kings of Ireland. The main theme in these tales is Ireland, represented as a goddess, and the hero of the tale is considering marrying her. This cycle featured Irish kings, some good and some bad.

The Celts let their imagination run free as they created some of the most fascinating pieces of literature the world has ever seen. These legends remain an inspiration for modern Druids and the literary world to this day.

Chapter 6: The Druid's Toolkit

In this chapter, we will look at what modern druids need to hold a ritual and express their Druidic philosophy. We'll go through the various tools needed to perform rituals, like a wand, staff, crane bag, druid egg, druid cord, and sickle. We also provide some DIY tips for creating some of these tools.

The main function of a Druid bag is to hold your ritual tools.
https://unsplash.com/photos/EtyuHwCSsn0

Druid Tools

The exact purpose of Druid tools remains a mystery since there are no written records about Druid practices. If you want to start practicing Druidism, you may be wondering about the kind of items you must get. The truth is that you may not need any. You already possess the energy required to perform different rituals. However, you are free to include certain tools in your practice, and the following are the most common tools.

Staff (or Rod)

A staff or rod is regarded as a personal tool because no one is allowed to touch it apart from the owner. Staff and rods are made from wood which transfers power from the owner to the tool. The power of the rod is determined by the type of tree and its location. Wands can also be used in place of staff or rods.

It is usually between three and six feet and is mainly used for protection. It also symbolizes position or power in society. When you place the rod in the ground and mark the shadow, you can calculate the area measurement. Religious leaders and kings are often associated with staff or rods.

The ancient purpose of a rod was to get accurate measurements of corpses for markings of graves. You can also use it to record the distance or journeys covered. Carvings were also utilized for that purpose. A staff is similar to a walking stick in modern times and consists of a longer rod. The owner can carve various symbols on their rod and assign meanings they understand. They can also decide the purpose of this tool depending on their needs.

Wand

Like a staff or rod, a wand is another personal tool in Druidism. The owner is the only person who should touch the wand because it is special. Although the wand does not have any powers, it is commonly used as a way to convey personal power. The user has the power, and it does not reside in this tool.

Crane Bag

A crane bag is a druid's special bag, and many Druids use them to carry different tools. A crane bag is used to carry a variety of tools like stones, magical objects, shells, feathers, rocks, Ogham staves, and more. This is a unique possession for each druid since it is utilized to carry all the crucial components required for performing rituals.

Sickle

A sickle is another tool used by the Druids, but its interpretation depends on how you intend to use it. A sickle can be used as a harvesting tool, and other Druids even use it as a weapon. Depending on your needs, you can choose your sickle's correct use.

Druid Egg

Modern Druids do not commonly use the Druid egg. However, it is mainly used for grounding by the user. It is made from crystals, stones, or other materials known as hag stones. Adder stones have a glassy appearance, and they have a natural hole created by running water. The stones act as protective and healing amulets, and they give the bearer some powers to see other worlds.

Because the stones have holes made by running water, they are believed to possess the power of water. As a result, they are said to ward off bad spirits. They can be placed above doorways, barns, milking stalls, beds, or stables to keep evil spirits at bay.

Druid Cord

A Druid cord is still used today, although it might not be mysterious like other Druid tools. Its main function is geometry, and it helps us create or map out sacred spaces. You can use it to create right-angle triangles for laying sacred items. You can make your cord like other tools. The following section will explain the measures you can take to make your own tools.

Creating a Crane Bag

A crane bag can be made from any durable material such as leather, skin, hide, wool, linen, denim, cloth, and others. Once you choose the appropriate material, you can make your crane. Creating your own crane bag allows you to personalize it by putting your own energy into it. It is believed that Druid tools don't possess any power but that their owner does. If you buy a used bag, you can also customize it by painting or decorating it the way you like.

Crane bags are meant for various purposes. When making your bag, you should know its intended use. The main function of a Druid bag is to hold your ritual tools wherever you go. The bags come in different sizes, and you can use them to carry your sickle, wand, elemental representations, and notebook.

The second option you should consider is to make a much smaller crane bag known as the power object bag. You can frequently carry this one because it can easily fit into your pocket, hang around your neck, or attach to a belt. You can carry spiritual objects in your bag like shells, sacred stones, herbs, sticks, bones, teeth, or whatever you deem crucial in your ritual work. You'll develop a strong connection with your tools when you always carry your crane bag. The items will give you power and protection when you move around with them throughout the day.

The third approach is to create a field bag that can help you when you are in nature. Apart from carrying spiritual objects, you can also use your bag to hold the items you can use for other practical purposes, like portable saws, knives, and other tools appropriate for foraging. The idea behind this type of bag is that you must be prepared when going into the wild because you'll come across many interesting things like food or medicine. You can also use your bag and the tools for activities like bush crafting.

The last option is to create a combination bag where you can include different items besides the ones used for ritual purposes. You can carry other personal items and ritual tools in your bag when you enter the field. The benefit of having this type of bag is that you can carry whatever you want without limitations. When you make the bag, try to create something comfortable.

How to Make a Druid Cord

You can use any material to make a druid cord as long as it is flexible. However, be sure the material is not stretchy or elastic. When making Druid tools, it makes sense to use natural materials like cotton or hemp, which are non-reactive and non-conductive. Create knots on your cord at regular intervals and ensure they are equal in length. Your cord must have 12 knots, and you'll end up with 13 sections you can work with.

The length of the cord should be one yard. However, it is meant for geometry and not for exact measurements. This means that the length is irrelevant. If you intend to make several triangles of different sizes, you can create many cords with different lengths. You can make triangles with bigger right angles with a longer druid cord.

Your Druid cord should be a functional geometric tool, so it does not need special decorations. Always remember the purpose of the cord when you create it, and carry it in your crane bag when going out into the field.

Making a Wand

Use wood that has fallen from a living tree to make your wand instead of cutting one down. Chopping wood to make a wand is often viewed as an act of violence towards nature, so you must use a piece that has been naturally provided.

A branch with a natural spiral is fit for the purpose. For instance, a vine that creeps around the branch makes it perfect for making a wand, also known as a Dragon. If the wand is made from ash wood, it will be called an Ash Dragon, whereas Oak Dragons are made from oak. However, Oak dragons are rare because they are not common in all areas.

When choosing the type of wood to make your wand, be sure to get something that can communicate with you in a certain way. Pay attention to what you want when you come across a piece of wood that you think is appropriate for making your wand. Each type of wood is ideal for different rituals. For instance, hazelwood is ideal for divination and can also be used for making items like dousing rods. Making a wand using wood will help you focus on gaining wisdom, knowledge, and divination powers.

Apart from knowing the characteristics of wood, you can also carve other symbols or Ogham into the wand. It is possible to increase the natural properties of the wand by wiring crystals at the end to increase efficiency. Crystals can also enhance the wand's energy so that it focuses on specific purposes. If you want, you can use modern tools to make fancy wands. For example, you can utilize a wood-burning kit, but leaving the wood in its natural state is a good idea. Add any decorations by hand to suit your needs.

How to Make Your Staff or Rod

You can use several methods to make a staff or rod, and they're all correct. In other words, there is no right or wrong way to make your staff. Do whatever you like because somebody's fit might not suit your needs. Ash and oak are the most popular wood choices because of their spiritual links. Other types of wood can also make good rods, but you must define your needs first.

Be sure to choose the wood that complements the purpose of your staff. For instance, Cedar primarily provides protection. If you want to cast protective energy, the staff made from Cedar would be ideal. Additionally, the Elder tree is renowned for its sacredness and can be used to eliminate negative energy or seek blessings.

To identify the best wood for your staff, you must have an understanding of different trees. Define the intention of your staff and walk into the woods, listening to what each piece of wood has to say about your intention. If you are drawn to a specific type of tree, it means it is providing itself to your intention. Looking for already felled wood is a good idea, although you can cut tree branches once you seek permission.

You cannot wantonly cut trees since they symbolize life. When you take a small piece of branch from a tree, its energy will tell you if it is the right choice for your staff. You'll feel the comfort and confidence that you are doing the right thing. When you cut a tree, you must do it at an angle and be respectful. Leave the wood for about 30 to 60 days to dry before using it to make your staff. Your wood must lie in an even position to dry.

If you cannot access wood from the forest, buy the staff from an artisan. When you buy a ready-made staff, be sure to do so with an open mind. You may find yourself with the challenge of choosing from a variety of staffs. If you are in this kind of situation, you must listen to your instincts and choose the ideal staff that aligns with your intention.

Whether you make your staff or buy one, you can decorate it or use it as is. There are no strict rules about decorating your staff. A plain rod is ideal for someone who is a minimalist. However, you can add decorations that resonate with your intentions. Carving or burning your decorations can be perfect for your staff, but make sure you have the skill to do it.

Painting your staff or staining it with ink is another great way of decorating it. You can remove the tree bark or leave it on your staff, depending on how you want to use it. When removing the bark, you must use beeswax or any other natural conditioner to condition your staff to prevent cracking.

You can also add items that include stones, crystals, antlers, bones, feathers, or shells to decorate your rod. All the items you add to your staff must complement the wood for the best results. Create grooves on the wood to affix stones to prevent them from falling off. Some people use adhesives or copper wire to add decorations to their rods.

If you are interested in practicing Druidism, you must have the appropriate tools. However, these tools don't possess energy. It's you who can energize different items utilized for Druid practices. The good thing about these tools is that you can customize them to suit your needs. There are no strict requirements about the appearance of the things you want to include in your toolkit.

Chapter 7: Working with the Awen

The Celtic culture is rich with symbols and energy work that serve one's divine and spiritual experiences. Awen is one of the Celtic world's most prominent and popular symbols. To put it simply, Awen brings inspiration and creative flow to those who seek it.

Awen is one of the Celtic world's most prominent and popular symbols.
https://commons.wikimedia.org/wiki/File:Awen_symbol_final.svg

This symbol has been part of Celtic rituals for centuries now. However, it has resurfaced, and people are now learning about it again.

In this chapter, you'll be introduced to Awen's origins and history. You will also thoroughly understand the deep meanings behind this symbol. It is important to know that there is more than what appears on the surface with this sign.

Lastly, if you are interested in integrating Awen's energy into your life, then you are in for a treat. You will learn different methods that will show you how you can be in tune with this energy so that you can learn how to manipulate it and work with it.

Meaning

Awen is a Welsh word that does not have an English translation. However, people loosely translated the word to "flowing spirit." It is said that Awen is a feminine noun and that it should not be confused with its deity, Cerridwen. Awen is a word that is always used in Druidism and is highly regarded and considered sacred. Its very vowels are considered divine, and Druids believe in their magical properties.

Druids like to begin their rituals by stretching the word Awen and singing it instead of swiftly uttering it. So then, the word is stretched into three syllables and pronounced: "Ah-oo-wen." According to the Druid ideology, the very letters of the word are magical. So when they are stretched enough, practitioners begin feeling the mystical effect of the word.

Celtic Lore of Awen

According to Celtic mythology, Cerridwen is the Awen deity. She is a witch goddess who is considered to be the mother who birthed all witches. She is also referred to as the initiator, muse, mother of Awen, and the keeper of the cauldron. The story begins with Cerridwen brewing a potion that will give her son beautiful features instead of his harsh looks. She assigned Gwion Bach, a young boy, to stir the potion that was Awen.

The cauldron was to brew the potion for 366 days. On the last day, the potion that contained Awen was ready to be consumed. However, because Awen is its own force, it goes to the boy instead of the witch's son. Three droplets traveled from the cauldron's surface and landed on the boy's finger. The magical potion burned the boy's finger, so he licked his finger to self-soothe.

Upon witnessing Gwion's revival of the potion, she chased him through the three realms, woods, water, and sky. The potion gave the boy three gifts, shape-shifting, prophecy, and divine inspiration. The boy shifted to a hare, fish, bird, and finally, a grain of wheat. The witch turned herself into a hen and consumed the young boy. Later on, Cerridwen finds herself with a child. She bore the embodiment of Awen. Her son became a bard, Taliesin, and a prophet.

History

The earliest records of Awen go back to ancient Paganism. With the rise of European paganism, the concept of Awen spread through the Celtic culture. The druids believed that they could awaken Awen in anyone using magical spells and potions. The Druids regarded Awen as a sacred concept because it is creation itself.

Celtic artists called themselves Awenydd and felt the power of Awen within them at all times. According to historical records, the Awenydd appeared to others as people who were in a trance or under a spell of sorts.

With the rise of Christianity, the notion of Awen persisted, but it was not as popular. It was revived when the Neo-druids came into the picture. The romantic movement heavily influenced the Neo-Druids, and they believed that maintaining a connection with mother nature was the source of spiritual strength. Of course, they found Awen in nature and any form of art.

The Awen symbol that people now know today was invented by Iolo Morganwg, a Welsh poet and one of the Neo-Druids. He successfully attempted to transform Awen from an abstract notion into a concrete concept that people can easily see and understand.

Symbolism

The Awen symbol is made up of a circle that is inside two other circles. In this circle, three small circles are separated from each other. Three lines spring down from each circle.

As you can see here, trinity is a theme that shines through this description. The number three is sacred and divine in the Celtic world. Other Celtic symbols revolve around the idea of a trinity, and Awen is no exception. There are a couple of notions that Awen symbolizes. Here are a few of them.

Mind, Body, and Spirit

Your creative flow is at its peak when your mind, body, and spirit are aligned and healthy. People believe that they open the gates to the Awen energy within you once they are aligned. So in a sense, each circle and ray symbolizes your mind, body, and spirit united and aligned. Once this holy union has taken place, Awen begins to surge through you, and you can start to connect and create with it.

Earth, Sky, and Sea

As mentioned before, Awen carries a raw power with the urge to create, so no wonder that one of its symbols has to do with creation. People believe that each ray symbolizes the earth, sky, and sea. This makes a lot of sense because, without these elements, life ceases to exist. The three rays unite and create life, which mirrors the Awen energy.

The Triple Deity

The triple goddess, also known as the maiden, the mother, and the crone, is a well-known figure in various spiritual beliefs and practices. Though this goddess is mainly founded in pagan and neo-pagan faiths, the Neo-Druids believe that the Awan symbol also symbolizes this goddess.

The triple goddess has three forms, but ultimately she is one deity. This can be seen in the Awen symbol. The goddess has three forms, but in the end, the three forms are in unity, together in the same circle.

The Genders

The Druids believe that Awen also stands for harmony between the genders. One circle represents the woman, the second is neutral, and the third represents the man. The second circle represents the harmony between both genders. With woman, man, and harmony uniting them, the power of creation rises to the surface, and the possibilities for the pair become endless.

Eternity

The Neo-Druids regard the infinite loops as the three elements of creation. On the other hand, the ancient Druids saw the circles as the infinity of time. They believed that the rays are the flow of eternal time and how creation evolves with it. This explains how they viewed the relationship between time and creation. So long as time is eternal, so is creation.

Consciousness

According to ancient Celtic mythology, the Awen symbol represents the Universe's awareness of itself. It is said that when the universe gained consciousness. Upon its discovery, a massive explosion occurred in space, and this was when life began to take form. So then one ray is the universe gaining consciousness, the second is the magic that created life, and the third is life taking form.

The Three Pillars of Light

According to Morganwg, the Welsh poet who revolutionized the Celtic revivalist movement, the three pillars of light symbolize God's divine name, the origin of the alphabet, and the stations of luminary bodies. The author of The Bards of the Isle of Britain, William Evans, explained that the three rays symbolize the stations of the sun and their role in the 4 calends of the year (the first day of the month in the ancient Roman calendar). He further added that the angles of the rays suggest the position of the sun at the time.

Inspiration

Ever since the ancient druids discovered the power of Awen, its symbol has mainly represented divine inspiration. The three circles were, of course, seen as the three drops of Cedridwen's potion that gave Gwion Back his creative surge. Overall, they saw the Awen symbol as the sacred creative flow that gifted artists, writers, musicians, singers, and poets with inspiration and creative energy. It acted as a pathway between their ideas and reality. It was their muse that brought their ideas to fruition.

Other Awen Symbols

- The Underworld, the Earth, and the Heavens
- The three stages of humankind
- Nature, knowledge, and truth
- Love, wisdom, and truth
- Harmony and balance

Finding Your Awen

According to Celtic Magick, there are various ways to evoke one's Awen. At the end of the day, Awen is energy. It is a creative flow that surges within you. It will open new doors for inspiration, and you'll be able to maintain your creative flow. Often, people sabotage their flow with criticism, but when aligned with Awen, you will see how this force disrupts any negativity standing in its way.

There are a few ways that you can awaken Awen within you and become one with it. You can practice spell work if you are more inclined towards Celtic Magick. You can also try certain types of meditation that can help you attain a level of consciousness that resonates with Awen. At the end of the day, the path you choose does not matter so long as it aligns with you and leads to your desired destination.

Spell Work

Working with spells is generally a wonderful experience. However, you must acknowledge that you'll exert a lot of energy while working on your spell. It is best that you ground yourself before you exercise your magic. This will get you the best results, and you will not be off balance when you are done with your spell.

Usually, with magick, it is best to control and get a hold of your energy before you start working on yourself. If you don't do this, your energy will be drained, and you will most likely be tired after your spell. Look for the best grounding method for you and ground yourself before focusing on your spell.

Candle Work

- Like any form of magic, candle magic has its own set of rituals. With candles, the choice of color, words, and symbols matter. A white candle works for all kinds of spells because white is neutral. Orange corresponds with creativity and creation. If you don't have an orange candle, you can use white – or vice versa.

Now that you have your candle, carve the Awen symbol in it and write your intentions on a piece of paper. You can burn the paper with the candle and focus on your intention. After you are done, practice your creativity. Let your inspiration flow through dance, music, painting, or any other activity that will require creative energy.

Herbal Work

- Herbal magick is similar to candle work. Every herb corresponds to a different wavelength of energy. With that being said, here are a few herbs that work with creativity and inspiration.

1. Lemon Verbena
2. Angelica Flower
3. Nasturtium
4. Bay Laurel
5. Lavender
6. Rosemary

Place any of these herbs in your incense plate or bowl. Of course, placing it in a tiny incense cauldron will be more fitting. Also, if you want to let your inner witch or warlock out, then you can put incense oil on your herbs. Now, light them.

Inhale the incense and feel the power of Awen surge within you. You can chant the word and focus on your intention. It will also help if you visualize Awen's energy flowing within you, and you can picture everything that you'll be creating by using Awen's power.

Meditation

There is a lot of power in meditation. When you meditate, you enter a different level of consciousness, and the deeper you meditate, the further you go. You can enter uncharted territories in your brain and experience different wavelengths. This is a powerful tool that can connect you with Awen.

All you need to do is find a special corner and begin meditating. After your mind quiets and you focus on your breathing, you can begin channeling the Awen energy. Take a deep breath and envision the symbol of Awen. Picture Cedridwen's potion floating within you, giving you eternal inspiration and powerful creativity. Focus on this vision for as long as you can. After you are done, try to use this creative energy and feel it running through you.

Creativity is a beautiful gift that everyone is blessed with. Of course, everyone has a unique way of using it, and their creations are just as special as their creativity. However, divine inspiration is an element that is often out of reach. So, if you feel like you are missing your muse or you are having a difficult time finding your inspiration, then you probably could use the power of Awen.

Ancient and Neo-Druids believe in Awen's divine flow. To them, Awen is not just a symbol or an ordinary notion. Awen is life and is as ancient as the universe itself. It can be found everywhere and in anything.

So, if you are having a difficult time with your creations, you can try to channel Awen's energy and be in a state of eternal flow with it. You can try different spiritual methods to be on the same wavelength as Awen, and you can once more feel inspired and enjoy your creations.

Chapter 8: The Ogham and Tree Magic

Before you aim to build deep connections with trees or nature in general, you need to understand that this is just like establishing and maintaining any other relationship. Besides being a give-and-take relationship, connecting with nature requires a lot of time and effort. It also needs you to work on your communication skills and be a great listener. Unfortunately, many people only take from nature. They think that it's there to serve us and our needs, which is why the natural ecosystems have now been compromised. In this chapter, you'll learn how to give back to trees and connect with them on a deeper level. You'll also find out about tree astrology and how our personalities are similar to tree species.

Your tree will become the stepping stone of your sacred grove.
https://www.pexels.com/photo/green-leafed-tree-38136/

Building Deep Connections with Trees

Find Your Tree

To start connecting deeply with trees and put yourself on the track for greater spiritual work, it helps if you find a species, along with a specific tree that you feel drawn to. Since this is just like any other relationship you build in life, you'll often find trees that you can easily "get along with" and others that simply don't work for you. This is because each tree species works with different human energy or vibration. While this is not necessarily the most amiable species to everyone, you may be surprised to connect deeply with hawthorn. This is why there are no steadfast rules or guidelines that you need to follow when you're finding a tree. Perhaps you're thinking of a specific species you think you'd be able to build a strong bond with. Either way, you need to trust your gut, your feelings, and the energy of the tree you're approaching.

While there isn't a single method you should stick to when you're searching for that one tree, this is still an essential step in the process. Finding a single tree to start working with is the core of all your oncoming nature-based spiritual efforts. Your tree will become the stepping stone of your sacred grove, which refers to the many other tree species that you'll eventually start working with. After you build a deep relationship with your first one, it becomes substantially easier to communicate with other trees, whether they're of the same or of a different species.

If you still haven't found your tree, going about the process in one of both ways can make things easier for you:

- **The Deductive Method:** If you have a particular species or an individual tree in mind, you should use this method. Think back to your childhood. Is there a particular tree that you knowingly or unknowingly built a connection with? Did you read underneath the shade of a large old maple in the park? Maybe you used to enjoy climbing up that old apple tree in the backyard. Reading under or climbing some other tree might have always felt wrong or unfamiliar for some reason. If that were the case, the trees you started a relationship with earlier in your life might be calling out to you to reconnect with them.

- **The Inductive Method:** In case you don't have a tree in mind, you can use this method. You can simply choose a place, whether it's a quiet park or a forest, and find your tree. When choosing a location, make sure to choose one that you can easily access at least once or twice a week. Make sure that it's a quiet area where you won't be disturbed. For instance, a tree near a busy street or a children's play area won't work. After choosing your location, make sure to rely on your intuition and bring all your physical sensations into play. Try to take a moment to clear your head and see if a tree calls out to you. Take your time, and don't rush. This doesn't have to be an intense feeling. You just need to feel a strong connection. Once you find it, ask if you can sit beside it for a while. Listen intuitively and search for signs, whether they're internal or external, for approval.

Start Doing Tree Work

After you have found a tree, you need to start doing inner and outer work with it. There are numerous things you can do in order to connect with a tree. However, we recommend following these steps for the best results:

Step 1: Search for its face. The best way to communicate with someone is to do it face-to-face. As odd as it sounds, you need to find the face of the tree the first time you meet it. You have to rely entirely on your intuition for this process. A tree can have as many faces as your intuition tells you. Figure out what they look like and what they're trying to tell you.

Step 2: Start communicating. It's best to dive right in and start communicating with the tree immediately. Use external and internal signs to figure out what it wants to say to you. It can be hard at first, but you should also try to engage with the tree. You'll develop stronger intuitive skills through practice, and it will become easier to do it each time you try.

Step 3: Do Your Research. After you've chosen your tree, you need to learn about it. This would require you to find out its species first. You can use a tree identification app for that. If you're still unsure, take thorough and clear pictures of the tree. Make sure to capture both sides of the leaves and the part where the leaf extends from the stem. Take pictures of any nuts, buds, or fruits on the tree. Gather any scattered twigs or leaves, as well. Visit a specialist to help you determine what type of tree it is.

Once you know which species your tree is, start researching as much information as possible about it. Find out the role that it plays in its ecosystem. Was it used for any medicinal, nutritional, or other purposes in the past? Do we still use it today? Learn about the specifications of its wood and whether it's endangered. If it's not under threat, how common or widespread is it? Is your tree an invasive, naturalized, or native species? Does it possess any medicinal properties? This type of information can help you understand how humans used to interact with this plant. Learn about what we have taken from it or how we worked with it.

This step may require you to conduct more in-depth research about your tree. You must explore various cultural resources to discover that tree's magic and mythology. Make sure that you're reading about the right mythologies because some trees, such as Sycamore, come in various species in the old and new worlds. Upon reading, explore the role of the tree and how helpful it is to humans. According to legend, is it a passive or an active tree?

Step 4: Learn to identify the tree and its species. Aim to familiarize yourself with the tree's appearance throughout the changing seasons. Pay attention to how its leaves, bark, flowers, and buds transform over the year. Observe the habits and shape of the growth of the branches. Truly get to know this tree and aim to notice and point out other plants of the same species. Visit them and spend time with them too. Keep up your efforts until you can identify the species, no matter how close or far away it is or regardless of the season and the general circumstances.

Step 5: Visit it frequently. Supplement your research with frequent tree visits. You can't build a strong relationship with anything or anyone if you don't communicate with them frequently. Unlike human interactions, you can't communicate with the tree at a distance via phone calls or text messaging. The more you visit the tree, the more successful your efforts will be.

Make Tree Offerings

It doesn't matter if you're following those five steps or if you have decided to do a different type of tree work. You should always make an offering to the tree as long as you're working with it. Think of the tree as a friend who always gets you small cute gifts. You need to reciprocate their efforts! All relationships should be a balanced amount of give-and-take. When you're working with nature, aim to give before you receive anything. Humans have been exploiting natural resources from the beginning of time. If you want to build a special bond with a tree, try to do things differently. Here are some offerings that you can consider making (you can combine them, offer them individually, or make them during different times throughout the year):

- **Play Some Music:** If you can play an instrument of any kind, you can try playing for the tree. If you can't, you should try singing to it. It doesn't matter if you don't play or sing too well. It is the thought that counts, and this effort are usually well-appreciated by trees.

- **Grow the Offering:** Sacred tobacco is one of the best offerings that you can grow, particularly when wild-harvested. Save the seeds, grow the tobacco in your garden, and then harvest and dry it. Be sure to do all of these things yourself. You can combine your harvest with lavender and rose petals. Listen to your spirit guides. They may ask you to blend your harvest with something else. Allow them to lead you and guide your offering.

- **Go Back to the Basics:** This may be the last thing you wish to do. However, you should consider peeing at the base of the tree. Every day, you benefit from the body of the tree. You breathe in its oxygen, eat its fruits, and sit under its shade. You depend on it for survival, and it depends on you too. Besides the carbon we exhale, trees need nitrogen to survive. Nitrogen is one of their essential nutrition sources, which is why your tree will be extremely grateful if you provide it. If you decide to do it, make sure to avoid peeing on the leaves because great doses of nitrogen can be too much for them to handle.

- **Provide a Special Offering:** Some trees like certain types of offers. Since each one has its own preferences, you need to communicate and strengthen your bond before you can get a sense of what they live. Even if they sound absolutely strange (yes, they can be stranger than offering your own pee!), you should still give them a go.

- **Spread Around Their Nuts or Seeds:** Helping your tree propagate is one of the best things you can do for it. Harvest its nuts or seeds and spread and plant them around. You should definitely do that if your tree is a hardwood nut since these species are usually slow to propagate. If your tree is an invasive species, it already spreads itself around a little bit too much. In that case, you shouldn't help it propagate.

None of these offerings are materialistic in any way. You don't need to purchase anything and offer it to the tree. This is because everything you can purchase at a store directly or indirectly consists of a natural resource.

The process of production itself requires great amounts of fossil fuels. You shouldn't buy anything and serve it as an offering when working with trees or conducting nature magic. Offer something of sentimental meaning and value instead.

Carry a Part of the Tree with You

It goes without saying that the tree should mean a lot to you. It should take up space within your heart and mind just like your family, friends, and pets do. In addition to that, however, you may want to keep a small part of the tree with you. If you do that, consider leaving a part of yourself with it too. Trees usually willingly offer a twig or a dead branch. You can give it some of your hair in return. This way, when you can't visit the tree, its energy is still present with you (this shouldn't be an excuse not to visit, though). You can keep the twig or branch in your pocket or purse if you want, but be careful not to send it off to the washing machine along with the pants. You can also carve and sand it into your desired shape and wear it on a string around your neck.

Tree Astrology

Like regular astrology, Celtic Tree Astrology is founded on the belief that our personalities and behaviors are associated with our birth dates and times. Druids came up with an astrological system that blended their great knowledge of the cycles of the earth and their deep connection with trees. They believed that trees served as vehicles for endless wisdom. They thought that our personalities were linked to different tree species.

Birch Tree: December 24 - January 20

Birch: The Achiever

This sign is typically very driven and likes to motivate those around it. It always aims for more and searches for better opportunities. This sign never stops developing higher aspirations. Birch signs (and trees) are resilient and tolerant. They're born to rule, as they have no problem taking the reins whenever the situation calls for it. These charming signs have a soft side that allows them to bring beauty and light into empty spaces. They're compatible with Willow and Vine signs.

Rowan Tree: January 21 - February 17

Rowan: The Thinker

This sign is philosophical, innovative, and creative. It is a witty visionary. Others often misunderstand its originality. The thinkers often master a cool facade even when they're feeling intense passion from within. This inner passion drives them to create their own path in life. Their presence can completely transform the people and situations around them. They influence others even when they don't notice it. Rowans get along with Ivy and Hawthorn signs.

Ash Tree: February 18 - March 17

Ash: The Enchanter

The enchanters are intuitive, imaginative, and artistic free thinkers. They are very moody and may withdraw at times. However, this is because their inner world is highly dynamic. They are aligned with their inspirations and muse. They are often interested in writing, science, art, and theology. Ash signs are always working on self-growth and development and seldom care about other people's opinions of them. They're compatible with Reed and Willow signs.

Alder Tree: March 18 - April 14

Alder: The Trailblazer

These signs can easily find their paths in life. They are always on the move and are filled with passion. They are charming and can get along with a wide array of personalities. They have a lot of loyal followers because everyone likes to be friends with them. The trailblazers are very confident and have a lot of faith in themselves. They don't like wasting their time as they are action- and result-oriented. They get along with Birch, Oak, and Hawthorn signs.

Willow Tree: April 15 - May 12

Willow: The Observer

Willows are very smart and intuitive. They are creative and have a clear understanding of cycles. They are patient and realistic, and they enjoy impressing those around them with their knowledge. Even though they have incredible potential, their fear is the only thing that holds them back. They get along with Ivy and Birch signs.

Hawthorn Tree: May 13 - June 9

Hawthorn: The Illusionist

The illusionists have significantly different external and internal personalities. Even though their lives appear average, they're incredibly passionate and driven from within. They are highly adaptable and can make the best of all situations. They are curious individuals who are interested in several areas of life. They're great listeners with a good sense of humor. They are compatible with Ash and Rowan signs.

Oak Tree: June 10 - July 7

Oak: The Stabilizer

These signs are incredibly strong, resilient, and protective. They stand up for those who don't have a voice. The stabilizers are generous and quite helpful. They have nurturing energy and have faith that everything will work itself out in the best way possible. They feel uneasy when they lose the sense of control over their lives. Like their tree, this sign can lead a long, joyful life when healthy. They enjoy social and familial settings and communicate well with Ivy, Ash, and Reed signs.

Holly Tree: July 8 - August 4

Holly: The Ruler

These signs are noble and regal. They excel in leadership and authoritative roles. They are always ready to take on any challenges because they can skillfully overcome them. They are naturally competitive and highly ambitious. The ruler is affectionate, intelligent, and generous, as well. They pair well with Elder and Ash signs.

Hazel Tree: August 5 - September 1

Hazel: The Knower

These signs are very efficient and organized. They are blessed with innate intelligence and can retain information easily. They are well-informed and have an eye for detail. This is perhaps why they need to maintain control. They are skilled in analytical areas and are gifted in science and numbers. Even though they need to maintain order, these signs like to make the rules rather than go by them. They get along with Hawthorn and Rowan signs.

Vine Tree: September 2 - September 29

Vine: The Equalizer

These signs are very unpredictable, particularly because they were born during the autumnal equinox. They are usually indecisive and overwhelmed with contradictions. However, this is because of their unique ability to see both sides of the coin. They are able to empathize with both sides of the story, making it hard to side with one. That said, they are sure about particular things, especially the finer areas of life, such as art, music, wine, and food. They like being around people who admire their elegance, assurance, and style. They are compatible with Hazel and Willow signs.

Ivy Tree: September 30 - October 27

Ivy: The Survivor

Ivy signs can make it despite all odds. They are intellectual, loyal, and compassionate. This sign is also very helpful and generous. Even though life often throws obstacles at the survivors, they face them with grace and perseverance. They are characterized by their charm and charisma and get along well with Oak and Ash signs.

Reed Tree: October 28 - November 24

Reed: The Inquisitor

These individuals like to dig into the hidden truth and meaning of things. They will get to the core of whatever matter they put their minds to. They like to hear all about lore, legend, and gossip, which is why they thrive as journalists, historians, and detectives. They are compatible with Oak and Ash signs.

Elder Tree: November 25 - December 23

Elder: The Seeker

The seekers are wild and adventurous. They seek freedom and thrilling adventures. Even though they are very extroverted, they tend to withdraw at times. This is why they are wrongfully misinterpreted as outsiders. They are highly considerate and try their best to be helpful. However, they are brutally honest. They get along with Holly and Alder signs.

If you think about it, the relationship between nature and humans is essentially a reciprocal one. All the things that your body naturally discards, such as the carbon dioxide that we breathe out, the nutrients that leave our body through our feces and eventually break down to enrich the soil, and the nitrogen that escapes through the urine, are all things that plants and trees need to survive. In turn, trees give us oxygen, food, shade, shelter, and a lot more. If we remember the foundation of our relationship with nature, moving away from a consumerist world, we can establish deeper relationships with trees.

Chapter 9: Druidic Rituals and Ceremonies

Practicing rituals is very common in Druidism. Generally, people practice rituals for spiritual reasons, and Druidism is no different. Rituals in the Druidic belief help its followers increase their awareness of the here and now and of everything that is sacred as well. Every action and gesture is symbolic and usually has a meaning behind it. They are meant to deepen your awareness and appreciation of everything life has to offer. The Druidic legends and myths usually provide inspiration for various rituals. You'll find that some Druidic rituals take place outdoors, in nature. This makes sense since the Druids highly revere nature and consider it to be sacred. However, you can also set an altar indoors and perform your ritual.

You can set a Samhain altar and decorate it with seasonal symbols and items related to Samhain.
https://unsplash.com/photos/twVS-YjQn9Y

Many of the modern Druid's rituals are usually practiced in circles to represent equality and unity. The circle is often a symbol of the planet, while the participants represent humanity. Rituals in Druidism are unique, and their main purpose is often to align the participants with nature. Druids practice various rituals, but the most common ones occur during the wheel of the year celebrations discussed in a previous chapter. They perform these rituals to celebrate the new seasons and connect with nature through meditation. Some of these seasonal rituals take place in a large group or a gathering of Druids, and they are usually more structured and organized. Each group tends to tailor its ceremonies according to the season; however, the rituals differ from one group to another since each group is unique. All Druids practice rituals since they all agree that nature is sacred, and they help them revere and connect with nature.

The Rites of Passing Ritual

The rites of passing rituals are one of the most common Druidic rituals. It usually takes place after the death of a loved one. Some people perform it on the same day a person dies, a week after their death during the cremation or burial, or at some time after the passing as a memorial ceremony. There is no time limit to this ritual as some can perform it years after someone dies as a release of their grief. The tone of the ritual can either be formal, joyful, or solemn, which usually depends on the wishes of the deceased. The rite of passing ritual can take place in a crematorium, a cemetery, or any historical or religious site. You can also perform this ceremony at the place where you will scatter the deceased ashes.

Before you begin the ritual, you should bless the space where you'll be performing the ritual. Purify the area and present offerings as well to make sure that the spirits of the place will willingly accept the rite. Choose an appropriate spot, draw a circle on the ground, and decorate it depending on the ritual. If you feel that a circle is inappropriate for the ceremony, you can build an altar instead. You can place all the items you'll need for the ceremony on the altar. It can also act as a focal point for the ritual. Place items like flowers, plants, pictures, or personal items of the deceased. For a formal rite, you can ask a priest or priestess to lead the event, as they will know exactly what should be said and done. You can also lead the ceremony yourself or get one of the participants to do it.

There are often words that are spoken during the rite that any of the participants can say. You can invite as many guests as you like, just a few people, or you can do this ritual by yourself. Now for the ritual, the participants should stand around the circle. The priest will welcome everyone then they will call upon the spirits of the place to guide and inspire the ceremony. The priest will make a call for peace in each of the four directions then they will ask all participants to form a circle that can be loose or tight. This depends on the participants' preferences. You should then purify and bless the circle with water and incense.

Afterward, the participants should all make calls to the four elements and the four directions to ask them to provide them with blessings during this hard time. After making these calls, the participants should now honor the spirits of the sky, earth, seas, and the spirits of place. After they are done, they should begin to honor their ancestors. Next, they should begin sharing stories of the deceased. They can talk about special memories of them, share funny stories, or express their grief. They can also take this time and simply talk to the gods. If words fail them, they can sing songs to express their feelings. Their stories and songs are considered offerings to the spirits. Participants can take this time to let go and don't hold back. It is a time when they can express their raw emotions about the loss of their loved ones.

The ancient Druids held feasts during their rituals and served bread and milk. However, in modern Druidism, you can serve your favorite food and drinks, whether alcoholic or not. The priest or any participants should bless the feast first by invoking certain deities or spirits. After the feast, the priest or participants will bid farewell to the deceased. They can also present gifts to the deceased by burying them in the grave or under the earth or throwing them in a fire. During this step, participants can play music or read poetry. Afterward, they should take a moment of silence.

Now the priest will close the rite by praising the gods and honoring the ancestors. He will honor the four directions and ask to unweave the circle. Finally, he will be the last one to leave after making a silent prayer.

Samhain Rituals

As mentioned, seasonal rituals that take place during the wheel of the year festivals are the most common Druid rituals. The first festival is Samhain, and there are various rituals that you can perform on this day. You can take a meditative walk somewhere in nature. Be mindful of your surroundings and let every one of your senses take in the beauty around you. Contemplate your life as you are, just like the leaves changing colors and withering in the fall to come alive with radiant colors in the spring. You are also a part of the circle of life with your death and rebirth. You are as significant as every tree or plant. You are also a part of nature.

You can also set a Samhain altar for the festival's duration (three days). Decorate it with seasonal symbols and items related to Samhain (or Halloween). You can use items like:

- Dried leaves
- Skeletons, skulls, or statues of ghosts
- Berries and nuts
- Root vegetables and pumpkins
- Wine or mulled cider

Winter Solstice Rituals

You can build an altar to honor the sun's return. You can place various items on your altar, but the most significant one is a candle representing the sun. The colors preferred for the candle are yellow, gold, or silver. Place symbols related to the winter on the altar, like cedar, wreath, yule log, or pine cones. Cleanse the altar using sweetgrass or sage. Never forget nature during your festive rituals. You can plant plants or leave food for animals to give back to nature.

The winter solstice takes place on the longest night of the year. Take advantage of this night and spend some time meditating on the new season and everything you hope to achieve in the new year. Winter is usually a peaceful season since more people spend time indoors, and the world tends to get quieter. This is a great time to spend focusing on your inner peace and growth.

Imbolc Rituals

You can perform an Imbolc ritual to honor Brighid, the Irish goddess of home and hearth. You can either perform it alone or with a group of people. Set up an altar and place items related to Brighid, like a doll of Brighid or Brighid's cross. You can also add items to represent the coming spring, like potted crocuses or potted daffodils. Red or white ribbons will also add a nice touch, and make sure to place a few candles as well. If you perform this ritual in a group, then hand a candle to each person, as these candles will represent Brighid. Last but not least, you'll need a bowl of oats and a glass of milk.

Now, stand in a circle to begin your ritual, and make sure that all participants are holding their candles. A high priest or priestess or any of the participants will lead the ceremony and will begin by saying a few words about Brighid and the cold winter. The priest will then light the Brighid candle and will say a little prayer. Next, he will offer a sip of the milk to Brighid. And he will either raise the glass to the sky or pour a couple of drops into a bowl that will be placed on the altar. The priest will then pass the glass to the participants so each one can take a sip. Each person will pass the glass to the one next to them and say, "May Brighid bless you this season." After they are done, they will return the cup to the priest.

The priest will now offer the oats to Brighid by raising the bowl to the sky and then passing it around to each person to take a small amount. As they pass the bowl around, they should say, "May Brighid's light and love nurture your way." The priest will then ask the participants to approach the altar with their candles. He will use Brighid's candle to light theirs while saying a prayer. After lighting all the candles, the priest will ask the participants to all take a couple of minutes to meditate and reflect on Brighid's nurturing and warm nature. Feel her warmth inside of you and reflect on how she protects your hearth and home. Now contemplate how you plan to achieve your goals in the next few weeks. Since Brighid is also the goddess of abundance, believe that she will help you realize your goals. After you are done, the priest will end the ritual.

Spring Equinox Rituals

There are various rituals that you can perform on the spring equinox. Spring is a time to be joyful and optimistic and begin planning for the future. It is the perfect time to start new things and let go of whatever holds you back. Set intentions for the new season by writing them down. Write everything that you hope to achieve, from the smallest goals like doing your spring cleaning to bigger things like personal growth. The Spring Equinox marks the end of winter and the beginning of the warm weather, where you'll be able to leave the house to go out more and take the world by storm. Set your intentions to prepare yourself for everything you want to achieve this season.

Beltane Rituals

You can celebrate Beltane with solitary rituals or group rituals. Celebrate the planting season and the land's fertility and plant seeds for a solitary ritual. It is better to plant the seeds outdoors in nature, like in your backyard. However, if you don't have a backyard, you can plant the seeds in a pot of soil. For a group ritual, you can perform a ceremony of the love and passion of the god of the forest with the May Queen. The ritual represents the symbolic union between the God of the forest and the May Queen. You have the option to either keep things tame or lusty. This mainly depends on the relationship between the participants and if your celebration is family-friendly or not.

Summer Solstice Rituals

There are various rituals that you can perform to celebrate the arrival of the summer. The ancient Druids and Celts used to celebrate this occasion by gathering healing herbs and plants. They believed that these plants were most effective during the summer solstice. You can do the same but make sure to gather some of the sacred Celtic plants that are associated with the summer - fern, Vervain, Mugwort, Yarrow, and St. John's Wort. You can also perform a group ritual where you form a circle with other people, share stories, sing, dance, play drums, recite poems, and celebrate this sacred occasion. You can also light a sacred fire and keep it burning all through the festival. The fire can be big enough so you can gather around it with your loved ones or simply light a candle. Another ritual is to set up a prayer tree where you can hang prayers for the people you care about – like healing prayers. You can also pray for the whole world, like for the end of poverty and hunger or peace.

Lughnasadh Rituals

Honor Lugh, the god of craftsmanship, after whom this festival is named. Use your own skills and create an offering to Lugh. You can sing him a song, write a poem, paint, dance, cook, or craft something. Set up an altar and decorate it with your crafts, like a painting or a written poem. However, if your talent is singing or dancing, you can put something that symbolizes it. For instance, if your talent is dancing, place an outfit that you usually wear when dancing. Place a candle at the center of your altar as a symbol for Lugh and light it. Reflect on all your talents and think of all your accomplishments. Take a moment and be proud of everything you have achieved with your talent. Don't be humble about it. Recite an incantation where you call on Lugh to inform him of your talent and how proud you are of it. Now take a moment and reflect on the talents that you wish you had or want to improve. Ask Lugh to share his talents with you to make you more skilled. Since you asked Lugh for something, you should make an offering to appease him. You can offer something using your talents or offer wine, fruits, or grains. Meditate on the offering and think of your abilities, whether you are proud or insecure about them. Then end the ritual.

Autumnal Equinox

A gratitude ritual is usually perfect for this fall occasion. Set up an altar and decorate it with autumn items like a candle (preferably green or gold), a fruit basket of apples, colors that represent abundance, pictures of your loved ones, and symbols of things you are grateful for. Prepare gratitude oil using:

- 1/8 Cup of any base oil
- 1 drop of agrimony oil
- 2 drops of vetiver oil
- 5 drops of rose oil
- A pinch of ground cinnamon

Cast a circle and think about all the abundance in your life and the things for which you are grateful. Abundance isn't always materialistic belongings; it can be your health, family, or career. Using the gratitude oil, anoint the candle and then light it. Express your gratitude to the universe, the deity you worship, and everything you are thankful for. Focus on the candle's flame and meditate while reflecting on the idea of abundance. Think of all the people in your life you are grateful for.

How to Set up Your Own Druidic Ritual

You can set up your own Druidic ritual and perform it alone or with other people. You can perform your ritual at any time during the year.

- Build an altar using symbols related to your ritual
- Form a circle or build an altar
- Honor the four directions, the sky, and the earth

- Purify the space where you will perform the ritual
- Bless the circle and everyone involved in the ritual with fire and water
- Pray for peace in each direction and offer prayers of peace to the whole world
- Present offering to the gods or spirits
- Pray, dance, sing, share stories
- Meditate
- End the circle

Although the most common rituals occur during seasonal celebrations, you can perform your rituals at any time. Rituals can help you connect with nature and yourself on a deeper level. For this reason, modern Druids still perform rituals to this day.

Chapter 10: Grove or Hedge? Walking the Path in the Modern Day

With the re-emergence of nature-based spiritual practices in Western society, Druidism has seen a resurgence. In some ways, this makes sense, given the context of what we know about the ancient Druids. However, if you search online for information on becoming a modern-day Druid, you'll likely find multiple definitions with various nuances of belief systems and practices to follow. While many of these sources are well-intentioned with good information – especially those coming from more traditional or historical groups – most fail to capture the essence of what it means to be a modern-day druid in today's world. Especially if you're contemplating whether to be a solitary (Hedge) Druid or to join a group (Grove), answering this question is the focus of this chapter.

Hedge Druids are often found in places where nature is abundant, such as forests.
https://unsplash.com/photos/Enhs8UrXEb0

As a modern-day Druid, you can adopt many different roles and abilities, depending on what you want. You can also adapt as you grow in experience and advance through life. As you do so, you may find that switching between the different types of commitments and responsibilities offers additional benefits depending on your needs at the time. Alternatively, there may be times when it is more beneficial to remain with one type of group rather than switch between them, or you can even choose to go at it alone. Let's examine both.

Beliefs of Modern-Day Druids

Today, the word "Druid" conjures up images of mythical beast-men who live in the wild and practice magic. However, this is not an accurate reflection of the modern Druid. Many people have a romantic view of Druids as wise and old tree-loving men and women in the modern world. In reality, they were a caste of priests in the Celtic culture. They practiced similar rituals and rites as other cultures, but their main focus was on natural elements such as trees, plants, and animals.

Modern Druids are interested in the spirituality and practices of their ancient counterparts. They believe that there is a connection between people, the environment, and their natural surroundings.

Some of the common beliefs among modern Druids which you can practice revolve around the following:

- Humans are connected to nature and should respect the environment
- People should live in harmony with nature and not interfere with it too much
- An energy or "life force" exists in everything on Earth
- There are natural spirits such as trees, animals, rocks, and water
- People who feel connected to nature are more spiritual than those who don't
- The human soul can be reincarnated into new bodies after death
- People should be open to new experiences, explore their feelings, and understand themselves better
- Druids should strive to be like nature, in a sense, and be humble and peaceful

What Is a Hedge Druid?

Despite their preference for solitude, Hedge Druids operate just like any other Druid, modern or ancient. They are associated with the natural world and its creatures and have a deep affinity for plants and animals. This means that they are often found in places where nature is abundant, such as forests or isolated islands. Being so connected to nature makes them naturalists and healers who care for the environment.

The path may be solitary, but it is devoted to the natural world and to benefiting humanity. By putting aside the ego, they work toward integration, becoming a part of something, a solo tribe without rules.

Modern-Day Hedge Druid

A Hedge Druid is someone who practices Druidism alone, a solitary practitioner. Philosophical or spiritual activities are more comfortable when done alone for these believers. They never have, or have *very rarely*, joined an organized group (Grove) for prayer, worship, rituals, learning, or activities with others.

Some Hedge Druids choose to live away from those who denounce the Druid belief system. While others choose to live extremely solitary lives for other personal reasons. Because of their location or choice, some Hedge Druids don't attend Druid gatherings or events because of their associations with pagan organizations, churches, or religious organizations. There is a reason for this. Some Hedge Druids don't like talking about their beliefs or practices with other people or being in an area where they are not completely alone. In terms of communication, some Hedge Druids choose to cut off all face-to-face communication. While ancient Druids could only communicate verbally or through the written word, modern Hedge Druids had at least the option of emailing or sending a letter through the postal service.

As you have learned, the word "Druid" today is associated with magic, trees, and various mythical images. However, this has not always been the case. In fact, the word "Druid" has gone through many changes throughout the years. Today, it is used as an umbrella term for anyone who practices nature-based magic or spirituality. In this sense, one could argue that anyone who practices magic is a Druid. However, it is also used to describe someone who practices solitary nature magic. This type of practice differs from others in that it does not require the person to be in a group or near others. The Druid can perform this magic from inside their home or any other place where they feel comfortable.

What Is a Druid's Grove?

Just as other religious and spiritual groups have their own groups, Druids have Groves. The word grove refers both to a clearing in the forest and to a group of Druids. And it comes from the tradition of honoring other members, nature, and the practice and belief of Druidism itself in a calm and empowering environment.

Groves meet in groups either at a member's house or garden. However, most often, they will get together in a larger outdoor area like a forest or a park. Besides participating in seasonal celebrations, Grove members will participate in ceremonies and milestones, such as naming a child, getting married, or mourning. And they don't necessarily meet on a Sunday as churchgoers do, for example. They could meet once or twice a month.

What happens at these meetings will depend on the occasion. It doesn't just involve worshipping. Instead, they will group together to initiate new members, perform rituals, and explain and discuss Druid concepts. In most cases, the meetings act as a social gathering, with everyone bringing snacks and drinks and chatting about their week or recent personal events.

It is possible to find groves worldwide with just a few members or even ones verging on becoming a small community. The attendance of some grove gatherings is open to non-members, while others are not. Each one is different. Some perform community-driven activities related to the well-being of individuals or town members. These include days out, educational or fun seminars, and volunteer work.

There are groves all over the world. You may not even be aware of one in your own town. This is because some groups don't want to be made public due to fear of persecution.

Famous Groves

Throughout history, forests have been seen as sacred spaces by several different cultures around the world. These natural areas are seen as a place for the divine to be felt most strongly. Many different religious groups, cultures, and societies have created sacred spaces in the natural world. Many of these places were later destroyed by outside forces or through conflict with other religious groups. These famous Druid groves from around the world still exist today and are visited by those who wish to experience the divine connection found there.

Waipoua Forest

The Te Matua Ngahere at Waipoua Forest is a famous Druid grove in New Zealand. The forest is home to the oldest oak trees in the country. There are many stories surrounding the trees, such as that they are the remains of a giant wave that covered the country in ancient times. One of the trees is known as the "Father of the Forest." The forest has long been considered a sacred space by the Aboriginal people.

Kumasi Forest

Christened as the Garden City of West Africa by Queen Elizabeth in 1940, The Kumasi Forest in Ghana is famous for its sacred grove of ebony trees. The trees have been used for centuries by the local people for their wood. The trees are said to be imbued with special powers.

Stonehenge

Stonehenge is one of the most famous Druid groves in the world. The site features giant stones that have been standing there for thousands of years. Many people visit the site to experience the energy they believe lies there. Archaeologists have found evidence that rituals were performed there even before the stones were put in place. While we do not know what the site was used for, many believe it was a Druid site.

Broceliande Forest

Another famous Druid grove is the Broceliande Forest in France. This ancient forest was used by Druids as a sacred site and is the setting for the tale of Merlin and Vivienne.

These famous groves from around the world still exist today and are visited by those who wish to experience the divine connection found there. The sites are important examples of how nature and religion can be interconnected. These natural spaces have been considered sacred by many different cultures and religions. These groves were often used for rituals and other practices. Many of these sacred sites were later destroyed and lost to history. Other groves continue to be used for religious purposes today.

Where Can You Find a Grove?

If you are interested in the beliefs of Druids and are curious about the history of this ancient society, you can visit a Druid grove near you. You can find one by looking online and visiting them at their regular meet-ups. You can also visit an online Druid forum if you want to interact with other Druids online. There are also Druid festivals held in different parts of the world. These festivals are great for learning about Druid history and meeting other people interested in the same things as you. You can also find Druid books on the Internet or in bookstores.

Starting Your Own Grove

Sharing your experiences with others can greatly support your future journey. You can meet new people, make friends and learn more about Druidism. You could try and form your own if there isn't one in your area. In order to start a Grove, you need two Druids.

Consider these factors if you want to put together your own grove:
- Groves need to be clearly marked. Standing stones or concentric circles of trees are examples you can use
- Consider a natural focal point like a lake, river, large tree, or rock

- Preferably, it should be in nature, or at least in a garden surrounded by plants and natural living things
- It should be away from other people for safe and effective prayer, meditation, worship, or just for general group meetings that won't draw attention from passers-by

Grove or Hedge?

Perhaps you feel a personal connection to modern druidism, or you have been exploring nature-based spirituality for some time now. The principles may even be part of your life philosophy already. If this is the case, then you might feel like it's time to decide whether or not you should continue down this path with a group or on your own. Don't feel compelled to immediately choose how you'll practice. It's up to you. Druidism doesn't have any fixed social rules. However, you might feel more comfortable on your own or with others. It's not uncommon for some Hedge Druids to start in a grove and then go off on their own. In the same way, a hedge Druid might join a grove if they feel like they need some social time.

Consider How You Will Practice

Rituals are an integral part of the Druid way of life, and there are many forms. These could include daily meditations, seasonal celebrations, teachings, and even simply spending time in nature. The most important thing to note here is that all of these can be done on your own or with a grove.

- **Daily Meditations:** This includes a simple act such as lighting incense while sitting quietly, reflecting on your day, and setting your intentions for tomorrow. It can also include more in-depth third-eye meditation
- **Seasonal Celebrations:** This includes a Samhain ritual (held on 31st October with a bonfire and communion with the dead), a Beltane ritual (to celebrate the beginning of spring and the awakening of nature), and a Midsummer ritual (for the summer solstice).
- **Teachings:** These are often ritualized with the use of symbols, such as a staff for the teacher, a book for knowledge, or a candle for the light of wisdom.

- **Spending Time in Nature:** This could include walks in nature, gazing at the stars, or doing yoga in a natural setting.

Why Druids Practice Together

When you learn something new, it can be helpful to have people around who understand the terms, customs, and reasoning behind those actions. Having a group of like-minded individuals can open up new learning opportunities that you may not have considered otherwise. Consider if you need a support system when starting out, even if it's just to learn more. When you practice with a group, you'll have the opportunity to lean on your fellow Druids for support. If you're more solitary in nature, perhaps the idea of a group setting turns you off, which is completely fine. It can be nice to have people to share your insights with. This can help you stay on track, continue down the path, and not feel like you are doing it alone. In this case, consider an online forum- you don't even have to participate in the discussion. This way, you won't be completely alone. Unless you really want to be.

Disadvantages of Practicing in a Grove

There are a few things to consider about practicing with a grove. You may find that you are constantly switching groups and never really finding the "right" fit. Plus, every group has its own set of dynamics, and you may not always get along with others. Time commitments could be an issue too. Attending meetings mean lots of time spent traveling to and from events.

Tips for Beginner Hedge and Grove Druidism

When starting out, it can be helpful to clearly understand what you want to get out of it. This can help you to set specific intentions and focus on your goals.

Here are a few things to keep in mind as a beginner:

- **Know Your Intentions:** Before joining any group, make sure you know your intentions. This can help keep you on track
- **Find a Group You Resonate With:** While you may be interested in many different groups, you'll likely find yourself more drawn to a few. This may be a good indication that those are the groups you should join.

- **Ask Yourself Why:** When you are considering joining a group, ask yourself why you want to join it. This can help you to pinpoint what you are really looking for.

The history of Druids is one shrouded in mystery. This is mainly because they did not write down their teachings. They only passed their knowledge down orally from one generation to the next. And because of this, there are no clear rules about how we should practice. This means the modern-day solitary Druid is a unique individual who has the opportunity to live a peaceful and meditative life.

Whether or not you should practice with a group comes down to a few different factors. The best way to decide which option is right for you is to explore both and see which one resonates with you the most. Druids are an ancient society with a rich and fascinating history. The Druid order is still present in the modern world, and you can find Druids at festivals, online forums, and groves near you. If you want to learn more about this ancient order, take the time to do some research. You will be very glad you did.

Conclusion

Spiritual practices evoke various levels of consciousness and feed your spirit. Celtic spirituality and Druidry are no exception. The Celtic culture is full of spiritual practices, magic, meditation, spiritual chanting, and so much more.

Like any spiritual practice, Druidism has a unique history, culture, notions, and practices. In this book, you have learned of the difference between the Celts and the Druids. Even though they may have come from different backgrounds, they still share similar ideologies.

You have also learned of the difference between ancient and modern Druidry. Some ancient practices and notions have been preserved in modern Druidry, and the Neo-druids revived others. With the knowledge that you have acquired, you can reflect on whether you resonate with ancient or modern Druidry and which practices you would like to adopt.

Not only did you learn about Druidry's ideologies, but you have also been introduced to everything they believe in. You now know about their principles, beliefs, values, the four sacred treasures, theories, Druidic branches, and Celtic mythologies and legends. You have also learned about the significance of their yearly calendar, as well as their sacred holidays. Of course, every holiday has its sacred rituals. You can practice these rituals on the same dates as the ancient Druids did.

Whether you picked up this book to feed your curiosity about Druidry or because you want to add Druidic magical rituals to your spiritual routine, this book gives you everything you need to know.

For the witches and warlocks reading this book, you now know how to create your own wands and other magical tools. You also know how to use them when you need to. Having your tools as a magic practitioner is necessary; after all, you do not want outside factors to mess with your energy. If you want to practice druid magic, you can create the necessary tools that will assist you, like a staff, wand, crane bag, Druid egg, sickle, and Druid cord.

If you feel like your creative energy needs a little push, you can try to awaken the Awen energy within you. The Druids believed in the power of Awen and saw its effects on various poets and artists.

As you know by now, sitting with nature is essential in Druidry. Try meditating in nature, and while you are at it, you can find a tree that resonates with you. When you find your special tree, you can start connecting with it and practice tree magic. You can start by making some offerings before truly connecting with your tree. Truly, this relationship will be beneficial for you.

All in all, it is truly wonderful that you are learning about the Celtic culture and Druidry. It is truly blissful that you want to connect with their ideologies, though it can be quite underwhelming since the world is not as it used to be. However, you'll find that practicing these ancient rituals and including them in your daily life will be uplifting. They might just transport you to the time of Ancient Druids.

Part 2: Norse Spirituality

Unlocking Norse Paganism, Shamanism, Magic, Asatru, Elder Futhark Runes, Divination, Spells, and Heathenry

Introduction

Norse spirituality is a religious endeavor built on Scandinavian beliefs and practices that predate Christianity. Norse paganism and spirituality date back to the Iron Age's Germanic peoples. However, these spiritual beliefs never stopped expanding and evolving until Christianity swept the lands of Scandinavia.

Most kings were pressured into converting at the start of Christianization because of economic and political reasons. While some people converted, others didn't like the idea of having to choose one spiritual path over another. This is why they decided to worship the Christian god and incorporate him into their polytheistic pantheon. This was one of the main reasons why Norse religious practices never withered away with time. Since the Norse found a way to amalgamate both religious systems, numerous Pagan rituals, lore, and myths were significantly influenced by Christianity. The opposite is also true.

Even today, many practitioners of Norse spirituality like to explore their own take on the practice. This is partly because many ancient Norse religions didn't leave written records of their practices; most of their teachings were orally transmitted, which is why there isn't a holy book you can refer to for instructions. Most of what we know comes from archaeological evidence that gives us insight into ancient Norse folklore, myths, deities, and religious practices. Roman sources and Old Norse manuscripts, created post-Christianization, also provides clues about their teachings. Snorri Sturluson's Prose Edda, the Poetic Edda, and the Hávamál are a few examples of these records.

Norse religion is a huge umbrella that encompasses many paths and branches you can follow. Some of these paths are community-based, while others rely on solitary practices. This is why you must consider your preferences and community when choosing a path. Even though some religious paths allow you to adopt the religion as a philosophy or adapt it to your lifestyle and the dynamics of modern life, others require you to follow the traditions exactly as they are.

Studying each of these branches in-depth would be impossible before deciding which path to follow. Fortunately, this book is the perfect place to start. Here, you will learn everything you need to know about Norse spirituality. This book serves as the ultimate guide to Norse Paganism, Shamanism, Magic, Asatru, Elder Futhark Runes, Divination, Spells, and Heathenry.

Upon reading this guide, you'll learn each belief system's origins and how it differs from other paths. You'll also understand the key practices of each belief system and come across step-by-step instructions on practical spiritual techniques that you can try out. The last few chapters delve deep into Norse runes, runic divination and magic, and Galdr magic, and offer hands-on methods to use runes and incorporate them into meditative practices, cast runic spells and charms, and conduct the High-Seat Rite.

This book is perfect for beginners and more advanced practitioners alike, as it is easy to read and contains both knowledge and practical instructions.

Chapter 1: The Old Norse Religion

The Norse are one of the most mysterious ancient civilizations in the world. The origins of their religion and mythology have often been debated since no literature existed from the Norsemen themselves prior to the Christianization of Scandinavia. Most elements in Norse mythology can be traced through Indo-European and Germanic parallels, showing that their religion had a polytheistic structure, including a pantheon of gods and goddesses similar to how other religions perceived deities.

The Norse are one of the most mysterious ancient civilizations in the world.
https://www.pexels.com/photo/wooden-runes-and-stones-scattered-on-wool-plaid-6739035/

Norse mythology is a complex and intricate system of beliefs that spans several centuries. It includes stories about the world's creation, gods and goddesses, humans, giants, and other creatures. The myths are often narrated in poetry to make them easier to remember by people who did not have access to written records at that time.

Norse mythology is an integral part of the Viking Age, being a source of inspiration for many people during that period. Their stories are still widely known today, and many myths have been adapted into other forms of media, including movies and video games.

If historians were to summarize the Old Norse Religion, they'd say that the religion of the ancient Norse people was polytheistic. Their deities were split into two groups, Æsir and Vanir. In some sources, these groups were portrayed as initially having been at war with one another until both sides realized that they each had the power to destroy the other (but not without destroying themselves in the process). The two most well-known gods in the Norse pantheon were Odin and Thor. According to Norse mythology, other races besides humans, such as dwarves, giants, and elves, inhabited this world. The Norse view of the universe is based on Yggdrasil, a mythical tree with branches spreading to all parts of the cosmos.

This polytheistic religion is complex and includes elements of shamanism, animism, and ancestor worship. Norse mythology is a rich and varied body of tales and includes stories about gods, goddesses, heroes, and villains. The myths are often told through poetry and songs. Also, Norse gods have many different roles in their stories; they can be benevolent and cruel or kind and vindictive. In some tales, they take human form to interact with mortals, while other stories portray them as living apart from humans in faraway lands. This chapter is a brief introduction to Norse mythology and religion. It expands on the origin of the Old Norse Religion and beliefs. Despite being forgotten during the Christianization of Scandinavia, it remains one of the most popular religions in the world.

Origin

The origin of the Norse religion is a complex one. It developed during the Iron Age when the Norsemen settled in Scandinavia and began interacting with their neighbors. As they did so, they started to adopt elements of their neighbors' religions. The Vikings were among the last people in

Europe to convert to Christianity, and this process was not peaceful. The religion we know as Norse mythology today results from centuries of interaction between different cultures and religions. It is believed that the Norse people adopted many of their gods from the Germanic tribes living in Scandinavia then.

Iron Age

The earliest evidence of Norse religion comes from the Iron Age. Archaeologists have found numerous artifacts that suggest the existence of a religion. The Norse worldview was a development of earlier Germanic religions. Many motifs associated with the sun, including wheel crosses and imagery associated with solar worship, appeared in Iron Age Scandinavia. The Vikings held beliefs in spirits and magic, which are now thought to have been abandoned by the people of Scandinavia during the fifth century B.C., only to be revived centuries later when Viking culture came into prominence. The Germanic languages developed over several hundred years, starting about 1,000 B.C.E in what is now Denmark and spreading to neighboring lands as well. The archaeologist Gabriel Turville-Petre, among others, has suggested that early Scandinavian accounts by Tacitus offer some valuable insights into later Norse religious practices. Tacitus describes the Germanic peoples as having priests who officiated at sacred sites. He also notes that they have a hierarchical structure involving seasonal sacrifices and feasts.

Viking Age Expansion

Vikings, the people of Scandinavia, left their home countries and settled in other parts of Northwestern Europe. The populations of some areas, like Iceland and the Orkney and Shetland Islands in Scotland, were relatively low. The Viking settlers greatly influenced the Scandinavian religious beliefs of people living in Iceland. When Norwegian settlers arrived, they brought with them their god Thor, the most popular deity among them. According to some saga accounts, Freyr was also worshipped by some of the settlers.

Odin's role in Icelandic society was less prominent than it was elsewhere. Unlike other Nordic countries, Iceland lacked a royal family or central government to enforce religious adherence. Instead, multiple communities had differing beliefs from the time of its first settlement. In the late ninth century, Scandinavian settlers brought their religion to

Britain. The English church felt the need to convert the population that had immigrated with Old Norse names referencing ancient religious entities such as alfr and skratii (elves and demons).

Decline Due to Christianization

By the time Christianity reached Scandinavia, it had already been established as a major religion in Europe. While a wealth of sources documents the Christianization of Scandinavia, historians have had difficulty understanding this process because few narratives describe how Scandinavian society was converted.

When Christian missionaries from the British Isles traveled to northern Europe in the eighth century, King Charlemagne encouraged them to bring their religion and its accompanying culture and customs to his own people in Denmark. King Horik altered the religious practices of his country when he came into power.

During his visit to England, King Hákon the Good of Norway converted to Christianity. Upon his return to Norway, he encouraged Christian priests to preach among the population. However, this angered some members of the pagan community, who burned three churches in Trondheim to protest what they saw as an unwanted foreign influence. Norwegian resistance to Christianity continued under his successor Harald Greycloak. Under pressure from the Danish king, Haakon Sigurdsson agreed to be baptized and allowed Christians to preach in Norway. Although Christianization had progressed steadily throughout Norway during Haakon's reign, he continued to support pagan sacrificial customs and asserted the superiority of traditional deities. During this era, the Norsemen's native pagan beliefs were transformed into a unique combination of Christian and pre-Christian practices.

After the death of Haakon in 995, Olaf Tryggvason took over. He was determined to convert members of the Norwegian upper classes. He destroyed shrines and killed those he believed to be sorcerers. When and how Sweden became Christian is unclear, but by the early 11th century, at least its kings had converted—and a few decades later, it seems that every Swede was also part of the Church.

Conversion to Christianity provided the upper classes and kings with support from Christian rulers in the form of capital, goods, and military support. Even though mass conversions became the norm, the Christian missionaries found it challenging to convince religious Norse followers to accept Christianity. As mentioned, the Norse religion is polytheistic and revolves around worshiping several gods and goddesses. The followers of the Norse religion simply absorbed Jesus as another God into their faith. Christianity inspired new forms of pagan expressions, such as by influencing various myths. Because of their relative isolation, Scandinavians living in rural areas may have held onto certain pre-Christian beliefs for longer than those living in cities.

Post-Christianization Survival

Although paganism had ceased to threaten Christianity by the 12th century seriously, Scandinavian priests continued to oppose it.

The stories of the Norse gods and goddesses were passed down orally for at least two centuries before being written down in the 13th century. It is unclear how these stories were passed down to later generations. Some historians theorize that some pagans may have held onto their belief system during the 11th and 12th centuries. For example, some scholars believe that the old gods were worshipped secretly by individuals who were hesitant to abandon their pagan past. However, this theory has little evidence beyond a few myths about hidden witches and sorcerers.

The mythological themes of Old Norse poetry continued to be a source of inspiration for poets in the eleventh century when King Cnut ruled England. Saxo studied the ancient practices of his ancestors, not in an attempt to revive them but because he was interested in their history.

Snorri reexamined the myths passed down through generations, writing about them from a cultural historian's perspective. As a result, Norse mythology remained popular for hundreds of years after belief in its gods had faded away. Despite the prevalence of Christianity in Scandinavia during this period, pagan rituals were observed for centuries afterward. Today, Norse mythology is still important to many people and is a source of inspiration in art, literature, and music.

Beliefs

The ancient Norse religion was polytheistic and focused on worshipping a pantheon of gods, goddesses, and other supernatural beings. The religion was practiced by people living in Scandinavia, Iceland, the Faroe Islands, and parts of Britain and Ireland.

Deities

The Old Norse religion was centered on a pantheon of various deities. Some of the most notable deities in this ancient religion included Odin, the god of war and wisdom; Freyja, goddess of love and fertility; Thor, the god of thunder; and Loki, the trickster god. From roughly 400 - 1,000 AD, these gods were worshipped by communities throughout Northern Europe. Many aspects of Old Norse beliefs can still be seen today, such as the prominence of natural elements like fire and water in rituals and prayers. Even though much about religion has been lost over time, it remains a fascinating subject for historians today. Thanks to curiosity and modern research into these early beliefs, we can gain a deeper understanding of this rich spiritual tradition that was so important to our ancestors.

The deities of the Norse pantheon can be divided into two main groups, The Aesir, which is associated with order and justice, and the Vanir, which is associated with fertility and nature. The difference between these two groups can be seen in their respective attitudes toward humanity. The Aesir were said to be more remote and reserved, while the Vanir were said to be more approachable and interested in human affairs.

1. Aesir

The Aesir are a group of deities representing the principle of order in the universe; this group includes some of the most well-known gods and goddesses of Norse mythology, such as Odin, Thor, and Freyja. These powerful beings governed the different aspects of human life, such as war, weather, home, fertility, and health. They were believed to live in Asgard, a mythical realm that was said to be connected to our world by the rainbow bridge called Bifrost. Despite their power, many of the Aesir were not seen as wholly good or wholly evil. Instead, they were believed to engage in a constant struggle for supremacy over the realms and over humanity itself. For this reason, people during this time often turned to seers and diviners for guidance on how best to gain the gods' favor. Though the religion of the Aesir eventually died out, it left behind a rich legacy of mythology that continues to fascinate us today.

2. Vanir

The Old Norse religion was centered on a complex network of gods and goddesses, known collectively as the Vanir. The Vanir were associated with nature and fertility and played a crucial role in Norse mythology. Some of the most well-known figures from this pantheon include Njord,

Freyr, Freyja, and Skadi. Each of these deities had its powers and areas of influence, but together, they formed a more extensive spiritual system deeply rooted in animism and mysticism. Despite its decline during the Christianization of Scandinavia, this ancient belief system had a lasting impact on Nordic culture, influencing everything from art and architecture to mythology and folklore. Today, many modern practitioners have embraced the Vanir as ancestors or guides in their spiritual journeys. Ultimately, the strength and resilience of this enduring faith are a testament to its timelessness and power.

Odin

The Norse pantheon was home to an array of powerful and complex gods believed to have played a crucial role in shaping the landscape and events of the world. One of the most significant figures in this pantheon was Odin, a powerful god who was represented as a mysterious bearded man wielding a spear. He was associated with many critical aspects of life and death, from wisdom and war to poetry and magic. He was said to have created the first humans from two trees and welcomed dead warriors into the warriors' heaven, Valhalla. In many ways, Odin embodied all that the ancient Norse people valued. His great power made him an object of reverence and fear, but he also had great kindness when it came to those who honored him properly. Ultimately, his wisdom made him the most influential member of the Norse pantheon.

Ragnarök

Ragnarök, or the twilight of the gods, is a significant event in Norse mythology that has captured the imagination of people all over the world. The story goes that an epic battle will occur between the gods and their enemies, ultimately destroying all things. However, many believe that Ragnarök may be more than just a myth. Some scholars have speculated that it represents an ecological cataclysm brought about by humanity's damaging impact on the natural world. Others see it as a metaphor for our impending death or a coming cultural shift. Regardless of what Ragnarök may signify, one thing is clear, this compelling story has inspired generations of people with its vivid imagery and vast implications. It is truly an enduring legend, both mysterious and inspiring.

Afterlife

In Norse mythology, the afterlife was known as the realm of Helheim. This was not considered a place of punishment or suffering, but instead, a place where souls would be reunited with loved ones and spend eternity in peace. According to legend, Helheim was ruled over by the goddess Hel, who had control over all mortal souls that made their way there. She would grant each soul whatever level of joy or bliss it craved for eternity, making no distinction between those who had lived noble lives and those who had been cruel or wicked during their time on Earth. Thus, contrary to popular belief, life after death in Norse mythology was not a grim fate but rather a reward for a well-lived life. Indeed, many ancient Norse believed that choosing their path in life and taking responsibility for their actions could ultimately lead to immortality in Helheim.

The World Tree

The World Tree is a central concept in Norse Paganism, representing the connection between earth and sky. According to Norse myths, the branches of this massive tree reach up into the heavens while its roots grow deep into the earth, connecting these seemingly disparate realms. Not only does this image represent a profound sense of connection between all beings and all things, but it also underscores the importance of balance and harmony in nature. After all, if one side of the tree were to outgrow or overpower the other, it could result in chaos and imbalance. By embodying these ideals, the World Tree reminds us that we must always strive to maintain balance in our lives and our broader interactions with the world around us.

Asgard

Norse Paganism is centered on the idea of Asgard, a realm that is home to the gods of the Norse pantheon. According to ancient Norse belief, Asgard was located at the top of the world tree Yggdrasil, serving as a sort of paradise for these deities. Although comparatively small, Asgard held everything its inhabitants could need or want - fertile fields, forests full of game, rivers teeming with fish, and even mountains made of precious metals. At the center of this wondrous world lay Aesir Hall, a soaring structure built entirely out of gold and topped with a towering dome. For many years, Norse Pagans worshipped their gods in this majestic setting, drawing strength and inspiration from the splendor and grandeur of Asgard. Today, while few people still formally practice Norse Paganism, many still look upon examples like Asgard as sources of beauty and wonder that we can all strive to emulate in our own lives.

Midgard

According to ancient Norse tradition, Midgard is a vast plane containing everything from towering mountains and deep lakes to sprawling forests and wild plains. Within this eternal landscape lives an incredible array of creatures, from mighty gods and noble giants to fierce dragons and cunning trolls. To truly understand the world of Midgard is to understand that everything in it is united by a web of relationships that moves in cycles of constant change and transformation.

Norse Paganism Now

Norse Paganism is a spiritual tradition rooted in pre-Christian Northern Europe. Today, many people worldwide still practice it to connect with their ancestors and honor the cycles of life, death, and rebirth. Whether as a spiritual practice or simply for fun cultural enrichment, Norse Paganism is living proof that ancient traditions are still alive in our modern world.

Throughout history, countless belief systems and spiritual traditions have helped shape the world we live in today, and many people around the globe still practice Norse Paganism. At its core, this ancient spiritual practice is based on the cycles of life, death, and rebirth found in all aspects of nature. By honoring and connecting with their ancestors through ritual, teachings, and communal gatherings, adherents of Norse Paganism gain a deeper understanding and appreciation of these transcendent cycles.

Whether participating in traditional ceremonies or simply taking time each day to connect with Nature as a whole, these individuals understand that we must honor the past if we wish to preserve the future. So, while Norse Paganism might seem like a foreign concept to some people, it is an essential part of our shared history and one that continues to have a profound impact on us all.

Chapter 2: Pantheon and Cosmology

Ancient cultures didn't have the science or technology that we have today. To make sense of the world around them and their place in it, each ancient culture came up with its own cosmology theory. Norse cosmology is about the study and understanding of the cosmos. It is a fascinating topic that includes concepts like the Nine Worlds, the creation myth, how the Norse people believe the world will end, and the tree of life. Scholars owe so much to literary works like the Poetic and Prose Edda by Snorri Sturluson as it gave them a clear idea of how the Norse people perceived the universe.

Pantheon Roman Temple in Rome.
https://www.pexels.com/photo/pantheon-roman-temple-in-rome-2928046/

Norse cosmology is similar to the shamanic traditions in other European and Asian cultures. Yet, it succeeded in standing out and having its own identity. Many 0f its concepts are based in the otherworld – the realm of the spirits. This realm is usually invisible to the living. However, in some tales, both worlds overlapped with one another. One of the main concepts in Norse cosmology is Yggdrasill which was one of the most significant trees for the Norse people. They had an interesting view of the world, seeing it as a large disc with the mighty tree of life, Yggdrasill, standing at its center. The Norse people believed that the world was divided into nine realms. From the branches of the Yggdrasill rises each of these nine realms.

Yggdrasill (The Tree of Life)

As mentioned, the Yggdrasill has branches holding all nine realms. This tree exists in all worlds: the underworld, the physical world, and the heavens. The Poetic Edda describes Yggdrasill as an ash tree with three roots, and according to the poem, three wells provide these roots with water. Völuspá, a poem from the Poetic Edda, mentions the Urda or Urdarbrunnr, one of the three wells located in the sky. Three maidens tend to this well. These maidens are the gods of fate and are called Norn. Verdandi is the Norn of the present, Urda is the Norn of the past, and Skuld is the Norn of the future. These three maidens are responsible for the destiny of all beings. The whole universe depends on this tree; the world will fall apart without it. Hvergelmir, the second of the three wells, lies under the second root, which stretches to Niflheim, one of the Nine Worlds. The third root belongs to the counselor of the gods, Mimir, who is known for his wisdom. This root stretches out to Jotunheim, the realm of the giants. In fact, in the Poetic Edda, Yggdrasill was sometimes referred to as Mímameiðr, which means "post of Mimir." This indicates that the tree and the third well may be connected to Mimir. One day, when Ragnarok (the end of the world) arrives, the tree will tremble as a warning that the end is here.

The branches of Yggdrasill stretch out over the whole world while the roots stretch throughout different realms. The first root stretches to Midgard (the physical realm), the second root stretches to Utgard (the realm of the giants), and the third root stretches to Hel (the underworld). The name Yggdrasill is believed to mean "Horse of Odin." The first part of the name, "Yggr," means terrible, which is one of Odin's many names, and the second part, "drasil," means horse. Odin is the main god in Norse mythology and will be discussed later in the chapter. Although the name Terrible isn't pleasant, it signifies Odin's power and how people were terrified of him. The tree's name is meant to honor Odin.

In the poem Völuspá, Yggdrasill is described as the sky's friend, and above the clouds lies its crown. Hávamál, another poem from the Poetic Edda, states that winds always blow around the tree. The Norse people believed that only the shamans could see the trees' roots before they died. They also believed that Yggdrasill was the sacred place where all the gods held their meetings. Various mythical creatures live near or around the tree. Duneyrr, Dainn, Dvalin, and Durathror are the four stags that eat the leaves of the Yggdrasill.

A dragon named Nidhogg lives around the base of the tree and feeds off its second root. On the branches stands an eagle whose name is unknown, and snakes are living near its roots. All these animals feed on Yggdrasill. However, the tree is never impacted, nor will it ever wither. It is strong and will last for as long as the universe lasts.

No one knows who created Yggdrasill, as it existed well before the universe or mankind came to be. It stood alone with the void before time itself. The nine realms were created around its roots when the universe was created.

The Nine Realms

The Nine worlds spread out from the branches of Yggdrasill, which also connects these worlds together. Unfortunately, Poetic Edda and other literary works don't mention the locations of these worlds or provide clear information or descriptions of some of them. The Nine realms were originally called:

- **Midgard:** The physical world where mankind exists.
- **Asgard:** The world where Aesir (a family of Norse gods) exists.
- **Vanaheim:** The world where Vanir (another race of gods that were known for their magic) exists.
- **Alfheim:** The realm where the Bright Elves live.
- **Svartalfheim:** The world of the Black Elves.
- **Jotunheim:** The world of the Giants.
- **Muspelheim/Muspell:** The realm of chaos.
- **Niflheim:** The world of mist and ice.

- **Nidavellir:** The world of the dwarves.

When Snorri wrote the Poetic Edda, he changed the names of some of the realms, merged a couple of them together, and added a new realm.

- **Midgard:** This one remains the physical world, but according to the Poetic Edda, it exists between Jotunheim and Asgard.
- **Asgard:** The Aesir Gods still reside in Asgard and are connected to the physical world (Midgard) by a rainbow bridge referred to as Bifrost.
- **Vanaheim:** Remains the world of the Vanir
- **Alfheim:** It became the realm of all the Elves
- **Svartalfheim/Nidavellir:** These are the two realms that were merged together and have become the world of the dwarves that exist beneath the earth.
- **Jotunheim:** The world of the Frost Giants and the Giants
- **Muspelheim:** This became the realm of a giant made of fire called Surt and his forces of chaos. It also became the realm of fire.
- **Niflheim:** The world of mist, ice, and now, snow as well. It also exists near Muspelheim.
- **Hel:** This is the realm that Snorri added, and it is the realm of the afterlife where the spirits of the dead live on.

Now let's take a more detailed look into each of the nine realms.

Midgard

Midgard is the realm of mankind. Ask and Embla were the first two people to ever exist in this world. Similar to Adam and Eve, all mankind descended from them. When Odin and his brothers Ve and Vili first created the first man and woman, they realized that these new creatures weren't as mighty as the gods or as strong as the giants. They couldn't live among giants as they would easily devour them, so they needed protection.

For this reason, Odin created Midgard so mankind could live, prosper, and be safe. The Prose Edda described Midgard as circular and surrounded by a deep sea, and on the coasts of the sea, some giants were given lands by Odin and his brothers. However, the gods later built a wall around this circular round world to protect its new beings from the giants.

The wall was made using the eyelashes of the giant Ymir.

Asgard

After they created mankind, the gods created Asgard, surrounding it with high walls to protect it. Before Snorri wrote the Poetic Edda, it was believed that Asgard was part of Midgard. However, his poems made it clear that Asgard is located in the heavens. The Bitfrost Bridge connects Asgard with Midgard.

. Odin and the rest of the Aesir (family of gods) lived in Asgard. A peace treaty between the Aesir and the Vanir allowed some Vanir deities to live in Asgard. Some of the most famous Aesir gods that lived on Asgard are names that you may already be familiar with, thanks to the Thor movies like Odin, Thor, and Loki. Asgard is a heavenly place with many towers standing tall. Odin's throne exists in a place called Valhalla, which is also a part of Asgard. Odin can see the whole universe from Hildskjalf. However, it isn't clear if Hlidskjalf is an object or a place.

Vanaheim

Vanir, another race of Norse gods, lived in Vanaheim. They were fertility gods who practiced magic. Just like how some of the Vanir live on Asgard, there are also Aesirs that live in Vanaheim as well. The Poetic Edda never gave any details of what Vanaheim looked like. However, magic and fertility were the main themes that defined this realm. It is believed to be a beautiful realm filled with light and magic.

Alfheim

Alfheim is another heavenly realm, and it is located near Asgard. It is the home of the elves, who are enchanted beings. They are very beautiful creatures who are creative and known for their love of music and art. Similar to Vanaheim, there is no accurate description of Alfheim in any works of literature. However, since it is the realm of the elves, it is believed to be as beautiful as these creatures.

Svartalfheim/Nidavellir

Svartalfheim/Nidavellir is located below Midgard. It is the realm where the dwarves lived, which is very different from the bright and lovely Alfheim. It is a dark place filled with smoke from the fire torches placed over its walls.

Jotunheim

This is the realm where Frost Giants and the giants reside. It is located in an interesting position near the two main realms, Asgard and Midgard.

There is a river separating Asgard from Jotunheim called Ifing. This realm, also called Utgard, is known for being a wild and chaotic place where magic is practiced freely with no rules governing it. The famous god Loki (on which the Marvel character is based) was born in Jotunheim. Like his movie character, Loki was the god of mischief and was famous for playing tricks on the gods. He is the reflection of the place he came from. Jotunheim was a dangerous place, so many gods preferred to stay away from it. However, some legends mentioned that there were gods who traveled to Jotunheim from time to time.

Muspelheim

According to the Poetic Edda, Muspelheim played a significant role in the creation of the universe. Surtr, the fire giant, lives in the realm of fire. It is believed that Surtr will be the one who destroys the universe, including Asgard, during Ragnarok. It is also known as one of the oldest of the nine realms.

Niflheim

Niflheim is considered older than all the other nine realms. This realm of snow and ice is where the universe was born. Niflheim is the coldest realm, so cold that no living being, deity, or giant can live in it.

Hel

This realm shares a close connection with the trickster god Loki since his daughter Hel is its ruler.

This realm is very gloomy and dark since it is located underneath Yggdrasill's roots. Odin was wary that Loki's children might cause trouble just like their father. He sent each of them to a faraway realm, and Hel was sent to one of the darkest realms. The realm has a massive wall that surrounds it. There is just one gate to this realm. However, it isn't easily accessible. It takes a long and arduous journey that involves crossing one of the most dangerous rivers in the nine realms. This realm later became the realm of the dead. However, only the spirits of the people who died of natural causes like old age and disease are allowed to travel there. It isn't mentioned in any literary work how or why Hel became a realm of the dead.

The Norse Gods and Goddesses

In Norse mythology, there are only two races of gods, The Vanir and the Aesir. The Aesir race includes some of the most well-known gods in

Norse mythology, and there is much known about them, unlike the Vanir race, about whom knowledge is limited to their realm and some of their deities like Njörðr who had two children, Freyja and Freyr. Njörðr and his children lived in Asgard. They first arrived as hostages but remained there to maintain the peace between the two races. They lived there in peace, were respected by all the deities in Asgard, and learned to work and co-exist together.

Let's take a look at the most prominent gods and goddesses from both races.

Odin

Odin is the supreme god and the most significant deity in Norse mythology. He is the king of Asgard and is often referred to as the Allfather or the father of the gods. Thor movies showed Odin exactly as he was depicted in Norse mythology, an old, bearded man with one eye. Highly respected by all the other deities, no other deity is as strong or as powerful as Odin. He is the god of war and death and is known for his knowledge and wisdom. Odin is very wise and has a thirst for knowledge. He even sacrificed his eye to gain more wisdom and enlightenment and reveal the universe's many secrets. This supreme deity is also the god of poets and has immense knowledge of the runes, which will be discussed later in the book.

Thor

For many people, thanks to the Marvel movies, Thor needs no introduction. The movies made him the most popular and interesting Norse deity. In Norse mythology, he is equally fascinating. Like in the movies, Thor is Odin's son, the god of thunder, and he wields his famous and mighty hammer, Mjölnir. In some cases, Mjölnir could also bring the dead back to life. He is the strongest Norse god, which is why he is also the protector of Asgard. Thor is responsible for lighting, storms, and rain. Similar to how he is portrayed in the movies, Thor is big and strong but has a red beard and red hair.

Another thing the movies got right was that Thor is a real hero, more so than Odin and Loki, who are more occupied with scheming. He is fierce and courageous and never shies away from battle or from facing a dangerous beast. In fact, Thor enjoys fighting. Besides his hammer, Thor also has a magical belt called Megingjörd. As a result of Thor's power and many other attributes, most of the Vikings revered and worshiped him.

Loki

Another popular deity, thanks to Marvel movies, is Loki. However, Loki is exceptionally different from the movies; he never became the heroic character the movies made him out to be. Loki isn't Odin's adopted son or Thor's brother. He is often referred to as Odin's brother, but not biologically; they are more like blood brothers. Loki was a trickster god of mischief. He can shape-shift into any creature of any gender, and he often uses this ability to play tricks on the other gods to cause chaos. However, every once in a while, he helps the other gods. He is so witty that it's safe to say wit and trickery are his only weapons since he never carried a real one. Although Loki is never described as evil, he was behind some terrible events in Norse mythology, like orchestrating the murder of Odin's son Balder.

Freya

Unlike all the gods mentioned so far, Freya belongs to the Vanir race. She is known for her immense power since she is the goddess of fate and war. Freya also has a tender side being the deity of beauty and love.

She is the ruler of Fólkvangr, which is a heavenly place where half the spirits of the people who died in battle traveled. The other half went to Valhalla. Similar to her people, Freya is known for her magical abilities and has the power to influence people's destinies. In fact, she has the gift of prophecy, which she uses to defeat her enemies and help her friends. Freya has a magical cloak that gives her the ability to fly.

Norse mythology is fascinating with its several deities, worlds, and how the people viewed the world. However, it isn't just the world of the living that is filled with stories and excitement. The mythology of death and the afterlife is equally fascinating, about which you will find out more in the next chapter.

Chapter 3: Death and the Afterlife

Vikings were known for being some of the fiercest warriors at the time. They believed that there was nothing more honorable than dying in battle. Dying in battle was their way into Valhalla, the Viking's equivalent to heaven. For this reason, they fought courageously and fearlessly in the hopes of reaching it after death.

In every religion or set of beliefs, people have their own idea of the soul and what happens to it after death.
https://www.pexels.com/photo/table-setting-with-lighted-candles-and-flowers-7705408/

This chapter will focus on the Norse people's beliefs about the soul, death, and the afterlife.

The Concept of the Soul in Norse Religion

In every religion or set of beliefs, people have their own idea of the soul and what happens to it after death. Norse mythology is no different. People often see themselves as having two parts, the body and the spirit. The Norse people, on the other hand, had a different view of the soul. The word soul in the old Norse language is *sál*. However, before Christianity, this word didn't exist. It only came to be when Norse people began to convert to Christianity. This shows that they didn't even have the concept of a soul before Christianity. What we call the soul, the Norse people called the self.

The self wasn't one single thing but something much more complicated. The concept of the self in Norse mythology isn't similar to how Christians or other religions view the soul or the afterlife, whether now or during ancient times. They didn't see the soul/self as just one thing but as consisting of various parts that don't necessarily correspond with one another. You won't find any of these parts familiar or similar to anything represented in Christianity.

The Norse people believed that four elements make up each person's soul/self.

Fylgja

Fylgja is pronounced as "filg-ya," emphasizing the first part, meaning "follower." The plural of the word is "fylgjur," and it is pronounced as "filg-yur." In Norse mythology, Fylgja was a spirit that mirrored one's personality and had the gift of second sight. The person and their Fylgja were very much connected and often had similar characteristics. For instance, a brave soldier's Fylgja could be a lion, while a quiet person's Fylgja could be a deer, and in very rare cases, some people could have a human as their Fylgja. Think of it like the Patronus from Harry Potter, which is linked to a person's personality and can look like an animal or any other creature that reflects their key traits.

Hamr

This word is pronounced like "hammer," meaning "skin." This element represents a person's physical appearance. The eyes can see the physical appearance since what the eyes see is usually real and fixed in reality. However, in Norse mythology, not everything the senses perceived was necessarily real. The Norse people believed that their appearance changed after death. The Hamr changed after death by either changing color or shape-shifting.

Hamingja

This word is pronounced like "*hahm-ing-ya*" with emphasis on the first syllable and represents "luck." However, the Norse people had a different view of the concept of luck than how it is perceived nowadays. Luck was just like honesty, courage, and a sense of humor, and it was a quality that a person developed or inherited from their family. Luck was what made a person powerful, wealthy, and successful. In fact, the Norse people regarded luck as a separate entity from the other four elements of the self/soul. A person's Hamingja might come back during reincarnation, which means it didn't always stay with them in the afterlife. Hamingja was passed down by family members to their descendants, especially if the newborn and the dead family member shared the same name. According to the Viga-Glums Saga, the Hamingja could choose the descendant it would pass itself down to, even if they didn't share the same name with their ancestor. A person could also lend a friend or a loved one their Hamingja during their lifetime if they felt they could use some luck.

Hugr

The word "Hugr" means "mind." It represents the personality or characteristics that a person acquired when they were alive. It is similar to the concept of the inner self. The Hugr stayed with a person even after death, which means that a person's thoughts, feelings, qualities, and everything that made them who they were when they were alive remained intact in the afterlife.

The Norse people believed that where one ended up in the afterlife differed depending on the person. One person could live on as a ghost haunting their home, remain in their grave for eternity, or reside in any heavenly realm with the deities. There were many possibilities. However, in some cases, not all the elements of a person's soul end up in the same place in the afterlife. Similar to modern and ancient cultures, the Norse people believed in the concept of reincarnation and that a part of the soul could be reborn, leaving the rest behind.

Reincarnation

Reincarnation is the idea that after a person dies, their soul is reborn and begins a new life cycle in a different body.

The Norse people believed in the concept of reincarnation. This was evident in how they believed that the Hamingja or Hugr would pass down to newborns from dead relatives. This means they believed that the soul, or at least a part of it, could come back after rebirth. Unlike in other beliefs, the gods in Norse mythology didn't judge the soul based on how good or bad the person's actions were when they were alive. The gods chose who ended up in their realm. It was either for personal gains, like in the case of Odin, or based on how a person died. What the person did while alive never factored in the gods' or Valkyries' choice. Since there was no punishment or reward, the idea that the Norse people believed that the soul could come back through rebirth seems plausible.

The Afterlife

The Norse people believed in the afterlife. They believed that the spirit of the dead would go to the otherworld, a spiritual realm. There were five realms that the Norse people believed the spirits ended up in after death. Here, we will look at these five realms and the meaning behind each one.

Valhalla

It means "the hall of the fallen," which was located in Asgard. Although the Poetic Edda mentions that Valhalla was in Asgard, there are other parts in the poem that suggest that it might be in the underworld. It was a heavenly place where the souls of the departed spent the afterlife. However, not all souls ended up there. Odin was the one who chose the souls that he found worthy of this honor. Valhalla is a place fit for heroic warriors. Grímnismál, from the poetic Edda, shows that Valhalla was built with weapons and gold. In each corner, there are feasting tables with plenty of food surrounded by the most comfortable seats.

Fierce wolves were standing by the gates, and eagles were flying above to guard them.

It is clear from Valhalla's description that it was a place like no other. It's no wonder every Viking warrior dreamed of dying in battle as they knew the luxurious life awaiting them. However, the Viking didn't spend all day resting and eating. During the day, they fought like warriors. Naturally, they got hurt and wounded, but they were completely healed in the evening. They got rewarded after a long day of fighting with delicious meals and an endless supply of the finest drinks. Odin chose the spirits' of these warriors for a reason. When Ragnarok (the end of the world) arrives, Odin will need a brave army by his side. However, according to legends, Odin and his army will meet their demise.

The Prose Edda details how the souls entered Valhalla. The souls of dead warriors who died in battle were the only ones allowed entry to Valhalla. Odin and the Valkyries chose these souls, but the reason was obvious: he wanted fierce soldiers for the end-of-the-world battle who would spend their time training and preparing for Ragnarok. Valhalla was the home of rulers, warriors, and heroes. If a person wasn't a warrior or didn't die in battle, then they would end up in a different realm.

Hel

Hel is a word from the Old Norse language that means "Hidden." This was another place where some spirits of the dead ended up, symbolizing the underworld. Loki's daughter Hel was the ruler of this realm. Since this was similar to the underworld, Hel is believed to exist beneath the earth. However, other sources state that Hel was located in the realm of Niflheim. It shares some similarities with the Greek underworld, one being that a gigantic dog also guarded it. Although Hel and Hell have similar spellings, the Norse underworld and the Christian Hell don't share any similarities.

Unlike Valhalla, literary works haven't provided enough descriptions of Hel to give us an idea of what it might look like. However, it was often discussed using a positive tone and terms when it was mentioned. It was a place where all the spirits of the dead, except warriors, were allowed to spend the afterlife. Hel was different from the concepts of heaven and hell that most people are familiar with. In other words, Hel was neither a reward like heaven nor a place for torment like hell. It was simply a place where people continued to live their lives after death.

However, the Prose Edda portrayed Hel in a different light from all the other literary sources. Snorri wrote the Poetic and Prose Edda after the arrival of Christianity, so he might have been influenced by the Christian concept of Hell. However, there aren't many scholars who agree with Snorri's portrayal. In his Prose and Poetic Edda, he stated that only people who died from natural causes like old age and disease are allowed to enter Hel.

The Realm of Rán

Rán was a goddess and a giantess who ruled over this realm. She was married to the Lord of the sea, Aegir, who was also a giant. The Realm of Rán was located at the bottom of the sea. The souls of the people who drowned at sea ended up in this realm. Her husband Aegir is often portrayed in a positive light, but the same can't be said of Rán. She would capture sailors with her net to take their treasures and drown them. Their souls spend the afterlife in her realm. In fact, her realm shone brightly as a result of all the treasure she took and kept there.

Folkvangr

The word Folkvangr means "the field of people" It was another afterlife realm located in Asgard and ruled by the Vanir goddess Freya. The Grímnismál from the Poetic Edda speaks of an agreement between Odin and Freya where they both split the souls of the fallen warriors, Odin took half, and they went to Valhalla, and Freya took the other half and went to Folkvangr. Judging from the meaning behind its name, it is also believed that Folkvangr was a palace for the souls of all people, not just soldiers. This was mentioned in another literary source, Egil's Saga. However, another translation of the name "the field of the army" could suggest that this was a realm like Valhalla that only accepted *dead warriors*. Not much is known about what this realm was like. However, Freya was known as one of the kindest goddesses in Norse mythology. She was a fair and generous ruler, and her realm reflected her true character.

The Burial Mound

In some cases, the soul didn't end up in any of these realms as it remained in the grave or wherever the body was buried. This was referred to as "the burial mound." Some souls didn't stay in the burial mound as they would walk among the living to haunt them and cause trouble.

The Norse Rites and Rituals in Funerals

Since the Vikings believed in the afterlife, naturally, they would prepare their dead for the journey. Some certain traditions and rituals were associated with their funerals. They would either cremate or bury their deceased. Early Vikings preferred cremation as a method to send their dead to the afterlife. They were followers of paganism and believed that the smoke would help the soul cross to the afterlife. The remains were placed in an urn, similar to what people do nowadays. A person must be buried with their belongings. However, they should be personal and specific items that reflect who they were and what they did when they were alive. For instance, a painter was buried with their painting equipment, a warrior was buried with their weapons, and wealthy women were buried with their jewelry. The dead in Norse mythology continued their lives in one form or another in the afterlife, so it made sense that they were buried with their personal belongings.

Some Vikings would bury the body or the cremated remains of their dead. They would either bury them in burial mounds, grave fields, or shallow graves. If you watch any movie or TV show about the Vikings, you will notice that boats were often featured in their funerals. Boats were significant in Norse mythology. They represented the safe journey a person took to the afterlife. The Vikings built burial mounds that took the shape of ships to guarantee that the deceased would travel safely to the afterlife. These ship-shaped graves were only meant for the wealthy. However, unlike what pop culture might make you believe, Vikings sending out boats to the sea with deceased bodies and burning them occurred on rare occasions. The boats at the time cost a lot to make, so setting these boats on fire every time someone died wasn't a viable option.

The Vikings dressed their dead in new clothes. They prepared specific clothing items for burials and funerals. It was important that the deceased enter the afterlife in new clothes to honor this occasion. During the funeral, they would chant, sing, and serve alcohol and food. The mourners would bring valuable gifts like jewelry or weapons that were then burned or buried with the deceased.

Ancestor Worship

Norse people highly revered their ancestors. Before Christianity, ancestor worship was a massive part of pagans' and Norse cultures' beliefs. Whether it was old or modern pagans, they all held their ancestors in very high regard. The ancestors were the spirits of the dead that the living kept in their memories. Their descendants honored and revered them hoping to get their blessings. The living never forgot their dead, no matter how long ago they had passed. One of their main blessings was the *hamingja*, a female guardian spirit that the ancestors bestowed upon their descendants.

Modern pagans, similar to the Vikings, still highly revere their ancestors and believe they can bless them.

In Norse mythology, death wasn't the end of the soul's journey; it was merely the beginning. The soul continued living in various ways, whether by living in any realm of the dead or coming back through reincarnation. Interestingly, living an honorable life didn't factor into how one would spend their afterlife; how one died made the difference. An honorable death in a battle was what secured them an entrance to Valhalla, where the souls spent their lives in the realm of the gods. The afterlife was a very significant concept in Norse mythology, which was evident by how they prepared their dead for the journey and how they were concerned about dying honorably.

Chapter 4: Asatru vs. Heathenry

Like most ancient traditions and religions, the beliefs of the Vikings and what we know as Norse mythology are dense and intricate. And, like most remnants of ancient cultures, it has been up for reinterpretation by contemporary practitioners who have found poignant elements that feel relevant to the present. Within this context, there has been a great deal of talk regarding heathenism and Asatru, two branches of Norse mythology and spirituality that have found a new audience. This chapter explores each practice in depth - its origins, historical background, and how it can be interpreted for modern life.

Thunder's hammer, the Irminsul, and the Woden's knot.
https://commons.wikimedia.org/wiki/File:Heathen_symbols.svg

Heathenism

On the surface, heathenism seems straightforward, but that's because anyone with a Judeo-Christian background will likely take the word for it to mean something else entirely. Others would easily conflate heathenism with paganism, even though they are very different concepts. Broadly speaking, both terms can be applied to anyone who does not follow the Abrahamic, monotheistic line of faith, with paganism encompassing a wide variety of indigenous and polytheistic religions worldwide. Heathenism is a catchall term to encompass anyone who does not identify themselves as a believer in monotheistic religions at large but who also follows the dictates of Anglo-Saxon spirituality and makes it their business to understand its roots in Norse mythology. To further illustrate the point, heathenry is part of Germanic polytheism, combining modern traditions with ancient Iceland beliefs. This entails the Anglo-Saxons, the Franks, and generally any ancient group that spoke German and its variants. The traditions of the Scots, while somewhat related, do not really come into play here. It's really all about codifying and celebrating the way of the Vikings.

Influences

Nowadays, when someone calls themselves a heathen, people tend to think of it in the derogatory, heavily Christian sense in that an individual does not believe in god or the prophets. The term has been widely used as a way to verbally bludgeon non-believers and ostracize them. If heathens could choose any other term to describe themselves, they maybe would. Unfortunately, the term came about due to a shortage of native words to help describe the myriad number of polytheistic religious beliefs and practices that were so popular in certain parts of the Western world before the advent of Christianity. "Heathen" is actually Old Norse for "heiðinn" and meant the "Old Way," signifying an attempt to hold onto the ancient traditions and beliefs of yore.

True heathens who wear the label proudly devote a great deal of time and energy brushing up on various texts detailing aspects of historical belief and practice. To really understand heathenism, one must also work to understand the origins and development of the tradition and how it came to be in its contemporary form. It is deeply influenced by Old Norse and Anglo-Saxon poetry, Icelandic sagas, early German literature, and even complex medieval legal codes and material as recent as 19th-century folkloric collections, some of which have anonymous sources. In fact, academic studies on archaeology and history also serve as critical primary texts for practitioners, which reflects a continuous attempt to better understand ancient traditions and ensure their practical application in the modern day.

Books, Books, and More Books

To better understand the origins and historical background of heathenism, it helps to turn to literature. The written word forms the backbone for much of the practice and how heathens form their own worldview. For the novice, reading could be a much more accessible and copacetic way of learning about the religion instead of getting involved in a local chapter right away!

One classic text that practitioners find to be inspiring is Padraic Colum's 1920 mythological tome, "Children of Odin." The illustrations are pure eye candy, but this book is primarily noted for how well it outlines important Viking myths and Norse spirituality. It's also an excellent example of how the work of more contemporary authors, practitioners, and historians has helped to influence a new generation of heathens by making these ancient stories more accessible.

Most people will tell you never to forget the medievalists since they arguably did the most work to collate all of the different practices, literary traditions, and stories, even as Christianity grew widespread in Western Europe and threatened to eradicate this important culture. Snorri Sturluson wrote Edda around 1220, which is an earlier attempt to compile Norse mythology. While this is considered an essential text, it is also known to be somewhat flawed since most writers working to interpret these traditions and stories often did so for a wider Christian audience, so there are vagaries here or there that can irritate more well-versed heathens. However, despite the loose interpretation of important cultural markers for the Vikings, the text is still an essential primer of religious beliefs and practices prevalent in pagan times.

Of course, poetry plays a significant role in heathenism and is a good way of getting more information regarding the ancients' cultural context, beliefs, and rites. One work that is considered to be a foundational text is Poetic Edda, a wonderfully rich poem that delves into the mythology and heroic poems of Iceland, drawing inspiration from a manuscript dating to 1270. The poems are intricate and magical, describing ancient gods and goddesses, the Valkyries, dwarves and dragons, and so on. There is something for everyone, and while it's definitely not for the newbie, it is an excellent way for those hoping to understand heathenism better to begin familiarizing themselves with its history.

Rites and Practices

In terms of their beliefs, heathens believe in the ancient Norse gods and uphold their important place within their religion. Heathens try very hard to uphold the rites and practices of the ancients while making them easier to blend into everyday contemporary life.

In terms of major celebrations, heathens hold feasts around what they call blots and occasions, such as weddings, baby-naming, or seasonal holidays like All Hollow's Eve. They also perform rites to honor different gods and goddesses or when they need to ask them for help.

Traditionally, a blot was a ritual sacrifice of an animal to the gods, which was then followed by a feast in which the meat was shared among the participants. A modern version of a blot still focuses on eating and drinking and paying homage to the gods. However, the ritualistic sacrifice of an animal isn't on the menu these days, and it's fine to have one indoors without having a major festival outdoors. Although, if one is to be had outdoors, heathens throw in a few choice items into a fire to pay respects to the gods and bring good fortune to themselves and their community.

A *symbel* is different in that eating is pulled out of the equation, and a ritual drinking ceremony is performed instead. Typically, the drink will be imbibed from a drinking horn, just as the ancient Vikings used to do, although finding an appropriate chalice is a viable option. Mead is the drink of choice, but wine could also work for most occasions. In a symbel ceremony, heathens could pass the horn around to all participating so that the drink is blessed and enough merry toasts are made to the gods, ancestors, and so on. A drink offering may also be made to the gods by pouring out the contents in their honor.

Beyond these major celebratory occasions, heathens like to make offerings to the ancients in everyday life to pay tribute to them. Heathens believe that there are "hidden folk" in the home, such as elves or garden gnomes, so leaving a bowl of cake or a pint of ale is seen as a kind gesture. These offerings tend to be left at a small altar in the garden that the heathen has made explicitly for this purpose.

Asatru

Asatru is a slightly different take on the ancient traditions than heathenism, but they are often confused with one another. One key difference is that Asatru represents more modern influences, reviving pre-Christian

Germanic polytheistic religions while emphasizing medieval Icelandic texts. This means that many of the ancient traditions are completely reimagined, and practitioners do not shy away from reinterpreting what some purists refer to as "classic" texts. Also, stressing Icelandic traditions and culture as opposed to Germanic history more generally accounts for the main difference within this religion. In fact, Asatru is modern Icelandic for "Æsir faith," meaning belief or loyalty to the major tribe of the Norse gods and goddesses. While practitioners usually refer to themselves as heathens, they will also openly share that their approach is slightly different.

Origins

This religious movement began in 1972 and was founded by Sveinbjorn Beinteinsson and a group of fellow Icelanders who decided it was important to bring back public worship of Norse gods and goddesses. Despite the once humble origins of this movement, it now has nearly forty thousand followers in one hundred countries worldwide.

It is important to note that while Asatruras do have a clergy, often referred to as *godar*. They do not have a central authority or dogma to follow. Followers of the Baha'i faith are the closest monotheistic iteration Astruars have since they also refused to make their religion dogmatic in any way, even as they believe in the central tenets that drive the heathen world.

Asatru has evolved since its first iteration in the 1970s to encompass a wide range of beliefs and practices essential to a modern way of life, including humanism and reconstructionism. They also tend to view the gods as metaphorical constructs, while others appreciate approaching them as distinct, powerful entities.

Three deities are widely believed to be the central organizing force in Asatru, Odin, Thor, and Freya. However, there is a large number of figures who also animate the distinct approach taken by practitioners. Also, a distinct feature of Asatru is that it emphasizes the importance of acting well and receiving rewards in this life, as opposed to waiting for the afterlife to reap any benefits. "We are our deeds" is an important aspect of Asatru, which is incredibly important to all its practitioners. As such, the Nine Noble Virtues is a vital part of the religion and serves as the driving force for all followers.

Nine Noble Virtues

The concept of the Nine Noble Virtues actually has a long history, and one version was thought to be devised by earlier heathens. It has been reinterpreted several times throughout history, but the last set was codified by Sveinbjorn Beinteinsson, the founder of Asatru, in the early 1970s. Broadly speaking, the Nine Noble Virtues are:

1. Courage
2. Truth
3. Honor
4. Fidelity
5. Discipline
6. Hospitality
7. Self-reliance
8. Industriousness
9. Perseverance

Later, followers of Asatru modified these simple yet arguably very broad concepts to include "Odinist values," which are more explicitly phrased moral or ethical guidelines. These are meant to offer some clear guidance on distinct moral quandaries that are not easily answered by the one-word dictates listed above. These Odinist values are:

- Strength is better than weakness
- Courage is better than cowardice
- Joy is better than guilt
- Honor is better than dishonor
- Freedom is better than slavery
- Kinship is better than alienation
- Realism is better than dogmatism
- Vigor is better than lifelessness
- Ancestry is better than rootlessness

Instead of residing solely in the world of moral absolutes, practitioners are given a very practical understanding of what's better than less desirable outcomes. There are other variations of these virtues as well, but in general, the central moral codes and worldview do not waver, and the idea is basically the same.

Rites and Festivals

There is some overlap between the rites and festivals that heathens and Asatruars enjoy, although the variations and intentions are clearly different.

For one, the blot is also an important occasion for those who follow Asatru but with a difference. While the blot here is also a rite intended to set out offerings to the gods, goddesses, and land spirits, they are also used to commemorate the dearly departed. It must be performed outside for dedicated followers, and an alcoholic substance is required. As always, mead is preferred, but beer and ale are also fine. In addition, the blot can be included in a festival held for a major holiday, such as midsummer or yule, and does not have to be performed independently.

The symbol is also important for followers, and the drinking ceremony is central. In this context, the symbol is perhaps less crucial than the blot, but it serves a vital function for followers since it is used as a way to establish one's identity and intent in a deeply sacred and traditional way. Despite the more flexible approach practitioners can take towards the symbol, there are a few well-established versions dedicated followers of Asatru take. In one version, people can drink three rounds. The first is dedicated to the gods, the second to great heroes of yore, the heroic figures from poems and sagas, and the third round would be an homage to the ancestors and friends who have passed from this world and have gone to the next.

Another popular way to perform the symbol is to pay respects to the past, present, and future. This ritual is meant to appreciate the parts of your past you'd like to mark, the things in your present you are thankful for, and elements of your future that you look forward to. Milestones, big and small, can be commemorated here in your own special way while also stating your hopes for the future. You can perform this sort of symbol with a small gathering of your closest friends or next of kin since it's meant to note something personal. While this version is less celebratory and more of a magical ritual, it is nonetheless important for followers of Asatru to perform from time to time.

Arguably the most important ceremony performed in Asatru is the profession. This is essentially a rite wherein you profess your belief in kinship and in the gods. It is usually performed to help mark an important moment in someone's life and state their understanding of their ancestors' power and earthly surroundings. This tends to be a very simple and short performance, but its poignancy is not lost on those who follow the religion. Even if it takes place in a regular meeting among practitioners, the simple act of loudly professing your beliefs among others is important. Sometimes the profession can be combined with the blot to help mark an especially important occasion.

Heathen or Asatruar?

Even though there could be some overlap, the differences between heathenry and Asatru are sometimes as clear as night and day. It's not really an either/or question, nor is one "better" or more authentic than the other. Both offer different roads for people to follow, especially those who are invested in preserving ancient ways of life. Interestingly, people adopt Asatru or heathenism for different reasons, and one reason could even be their political affiliation. Asatru has had an unfortunate moment in the sun lately due to neo-Nazis appropriating its central images and symbolism since anything with roots in Germanic culture is taken as a test for racial purity.

On the other end of the spectrum, you have a movement often referred to as "rainbow heathenry," which is a version that stresses openness to people of other ethnicities and gender identities and who engage in various forms of sexual expression without judgment. In this version, followers embrace a pre-Christian version of the world in which morality had less to do with sexual identity and more with ethical principles, similar to the Nine Noble Virtues described above.

Given that Norse spirituality is steeped in myth and symbols, it lends itself to interpretation by all sorts of people, which can sometimes lead to not-so-great results. That being said, there are hundreds of thousands of followers of both heathenry and Asatru throughout the world, and they are, by and large, devoted to the kinder aspects of the old ways. They are devoted to respecting elders and honoring the past while being deeply aware of the present. Many of us find ourselves unmoored by modernity, and technology has only hastened humankind's deepening sense of alienation. It's easy to get lost in the urban sprawl and the constant technological advances that are currently happening at breakneck speed, so it makes sense that people who find either Asatru or heathenry feel a tremendous sense of relief. They provide opportunities to slow down, listen to important tales and histories of the past, and create a strong, foundational moral core for people to follow.

Perhaps the main thing to note is that heathenism and Asatru should not be confused with Wicca, for example. Both, and perhaps especially heathenism, are influenced by literature and basic rituals, but magic rarely features in the equation. Furthermore, they differ greatly from most pagans in general in that they believe in each of the gods and goddesses as distinct entities and not as aspects of the overarching goddess whom Wiccans worship. They take polytheism seriously, as do ancient folktales and culture, and look for ways to bring them to life in the modern era. In all cases, these disparate groups have distinct theological backgrounds and differences, but they find commonalities in their shared desire to revive ancient practices that have long been suppressed with the advent of Christianity.

Chapter 5: Seiðr Magic and Shamanism

This chapter will dive deeper into one of the oldest magical practices of the Norse traditions – the art of Seiðr or Norse Shamanism. However, before delving into its background and, later on, the practical side of Seiðr magic, remember that shamanic practices take many years to master. For beginners, it's always a good idea to practice with an experienced guide who can teach you the basics of safe practices. Not only that, but they can help you learn to focus your mind on your intent. However, if you're unable to do this, whether due to temporary stress or an impoverished mental state, you shouldn't practice shamanism, as apart from focus, the process of Seiðr takes a lot of mental and spiritual energy. If your mental well-being isn't the best, to begin with, you won't have enough energy to successfully complete your work.

Smudging may be used to elevate the tension in your body and mind.
https://www.pexels.com/photo/a-bundle-of-sage-smoking-7947722/

What Is Shamanism?

Shamanism as a tradition has been present in human civilizations long before the Norse and Celtic cultures took over Europe and the rest of the world. Because of this, it's really tough to define what shamanism is. Evidence of shamanic practices has been found in cave paintings from the early Stone Age when the cultural development of human civilizations was still in its earlier stage. An overwhelming amount of evidence of similar practices came from the Iron Age when shamanism was already present in many different corners of the world. While somewhat similar in symbolism and techniques, the shamanic practices in each culture have already meant something different at this time. As human civilizations have evolved up until the modern days, so has the diversification of shamanic practices.

Shamanism is a set of practices through which one enters into an altered state of mind to journey to the spiritual world or contact one of its inhabitants. Typically, the journey or the contact is made with a specific intention, such as seeking advice, guidance, answers, and help with spiritual healing or growth. Other acts of shamans have included magical fears, visionary quests, weather working, shapeshifting, and divination.

How Is Shamanism Expressed in Norse Traditions?

Norse Shamanism has been practiced by the ancient Germanic tribes that had settled in Europe and, later on, the Norse people inhabiting Scandinavia. While very similar to Western Shamanism, the practice has been expressed slightly differently in Norse traditions. For starters, the foundation of Norse pagan practices has been built around the gods of the Norse pantheon, more specifically around Odin. According to Norse lore, Odin was one of the most powerful shamans. His work is evidenced in how he came upon the runes while hanging on Yggdrasill for nine days and nights without food, drinks, or sleep. It's still believed that Odin can help anyone enter an elevated state of mind and reveal the meaning of the runes. Odin's name is yet another proof of his ability to enter a trance needed for shamanic practices. The Old Norse word Óðinn is composed of the words "óðr," which means "inspiration" or "ecstasy," and the masculine suffix "-inn," which translates to the phrase "master of." When put together, these words mean "the master of ecstasy." Other myths suggest that Odin could also travel to the spiritual world before great battles to gather crucial knowledge he could use to secure victory. Other times he was said to make this journey for other people and deities while appearing asleep or being in a trance-like state. In a famous tale, Odin rode Sleipner (his eight-legged horse) to the otherworld to seek a seeress who could help his son. He would also travel to the underworld to consult with the spirits of the departed people and deities who have gathered great wisdom through their lives in the different worlds. It is believed that Odin relied on spiritual allies (often portrayed as two ravens) and taught the deities and people about the importance of learning from these guides. They showed him how to journey between worlds and gave him advice when needed, just as experienced shamans still do for beginners. Odin's trial during the discovery of the runes is also the basis for the shamanic tradition in which practitioners experience a symbolic death and revival before obtaining their abilities. However, one does not have to die physically and return to a new body. They could continue living in our world and travel between worlds even if they gained their power from a trance-like state.

That said, gaining runic insight was only Odin's first step in mastering shamanic practices. He learned the rest of the Seiðr from Freya, a goddess who originally belonged to another ancient tribe. This coincidentally highlights another notable difference between seidr and other forms of shamanism. In the early days, it was usually women who held this power. These women were called völva, seiðkona or seeresses. They would travel from village to village offering help, performing magic, divination, healing, and whatever was needed. Their spiritual guides led them to the place where their assistance was required. In return, they usually only asked for meals, housing, and similar forms of compensation. The few men who practiced shamanism worked in cults and were only concerned with wars, battles, and similar purposes, or worse, only with what they could personally gain. Whereas the völva looked out for the well-being of their entire community. Apart from healing and processes, it was their job to know how to find the best place for the tribe to hunt, spend the harsh winters, or plant the crops the tribe would harvest later in the year. According to Norse lore, the völva also could discern and shape the fated course of life of people by affecting it with magic. They would hang a few strings, pieces of shredded clothes, or plants and weave the fragments together, symbolically entering new, more desirable events into one's fate. Another way the seeresses prophesized was by spinning their staffs in their hands and entering an altered state of consciousness. Then, they would journey to Asgard or any other of the nine realms of the Norse world. According to certain myths, apart from bestowing blessings and helpful prophecies, the völva was also capable of enacting curses.

Another reason women were the only practitioners of Seiðr is that their abilities set them apart from the rest of society. While in most cases, they were highly respected (especially in the first couple of centuries CE), seeresses were also sometimes feared. When followers of other religions have begun to look into the shamanic practices, the völva often become reviled. They were forced to occupy less dignified roles than the rest of their tribe. Shamanic practices were often considered dishonorable, as were the people who practiced these. Men who worked with Seiðr were labeled as ergi (argr in Old Norse), which was a terrible insult amongst the Germanic tribes. Apart from the liberal way the women acted when traveling to wherever they felt called on, Seiðr was also considered ergi due to the weaving practice. Only women would want to meddle in fate and people's lives. It was considered unmanly to practice shamanism, which is why men were often shamed for it. Despite this, they are records of several men choosing Seiðr as a profession, presumably inspired by Odin and following his example. After all, the almighty Odin was labeled ergi too, but this didn't stop him from gathering a lot of power and spiritual wisdom. Some say that because of his shamanic practices, Odin could obtain the highest power in the universe. This knowledge was inspiring enough to disregard the ill-wishers who were only concerned with the current social norms and statuses.

Whether the practitioner of Seiðr was male or female, they were able to raise storms or invoke nightmares to stop their enemies and prevent them from entering into battle. They could also enact love spells and appear in the form of various animals to warn or guide people. When angered, the practitioners of Seiðr could provide false information about the future, make the land barren, and cause disasters. Journeying in an altered state of mind was standard practice and is one that has remained popular in modern times. One of the most popular acts of Seiðr is for the practitioner to sit on an elevated platform or within a sacred circle and enter into a trance-like state. During this, they seek out prophecies regarding themselves or others who require their help. Nowadays, more and more practitioners prefer journeying alone, although they do this after learning the act from an experienced teacher or spiritual guide. The journey often requires time for recovery afterward, as it can be exhausting for the body, mind, and spirit. The ancient shamans would also travel in the physical world, and not just when they were called. They would set out on a journey to find a source of spiritual wisdom, a better place for grounding, new tools, or whatever they felt they previously lacked. Sometimes, they needed to seek out a hidden item or information for healing, luck, or calling on the desired weather, animals to hunt, and so on. Other times they needed a new place for divination or a new ritual. They would usually take their trusted staff and roam the country until they were stopped, asked for assistance, or found what they were looking for. This is why they prefer to live in open places, apart from the rest of the people.

Another difference between the Norse and Western practices is how shamans enter an elevated state of mind. Western shamans typically require an elaborate ritual, complete with chanting or humming, drumming, and dancing, to elevate their minds from the mundane spiritual levels. In these cultures, shamanism is practiced in larger groups, even if it's only the shaman who does the journeying and collecting the information. In Seiðr, however, drumming, loud chanting, and dancing aren't necessary, although many practitioners enjoy singing and even a spinning motion. The act can be performed alone or in smaller groups, and the shaman relies most prevalently on their own ability to focus their intent on the task ahead. Some other tools they often use are a staff, a stool, or any elevated place for sitting, the spirits, and the spoken word (including prayers, songs, and chanting).

Techniques Based on the Seiðr Tradition

Modern techniques based on the Seiðr traditions vary depending on the practitioner's cultural and spiritual background and preferences for practicing magic. That said, below, you'll find the basic practices you can try to get started.

Cleansing and Other Preparations

Before you start any magical work, you'll need to cleanse your space, tools, and yourself. If you're working inside, a good way to purify everything is by smudging, i.e., smoking herbs with healing or other magical benefits. Besides banishing the negative energy from your working area, smudging may also be used to elevate the tension in your body and mind. If you're working outside, you'll only need to cleanse yourself, your tools, and the small area you'll be occupying (usually within a circle).

Prepare your tools - your staff, a chair for sitting, a blanket, and anything else you want to use. While a shaman's most powerful tool is their mind, you can use anything else that helps you focus on your work. After designating the area of magical work, you'll honor the cardinal directions, deities, spiritual guides, and nature spirits.

Grounding

Whether you're a beginner or an experienced practitioner performing an act of shamanic magic alone or within a group, the most crucial step to conquer is grounding. This means finding a connection to the energy of the universe and gaining the ability to harness its power. Seiðr requires intense focus, so you'll need all the help you can get. Grounding exercises will help you focus on your intent and form it in the first place. Whether you want to enact a spell, perform a ritual, journey to seek out information about the future, or do any other shamanic, you must root yourself in the present. Finding your place in the present will allow you to channel your thoughts in the right direction.

There are several ways to become grounded and focused on your magical tasks, and here are some you can try:

- **Using a staff:** Most practitioners use a staff to find a connection with nature and the universe. You'll need to find a quiet place outside and stand relaxed, holding the staff in your hand. Make sure it's upright and that it touches the ground. Take a few deep breaths, close your eyes, and allow your staff to channel energy until you find the connection.

- **Stomping:** Sometimes, simply touching the ground with your bare feet will be enough to make the connection. Other times, you'll need to put more effort into this. For example, you can stomp on the ground until you feel focused. The stomping motion activates your power and nature's energy and chases away any thoughts unrelated to what you're doing in the present moment.

- **Sitting on rocks and other natural landmarks:** These can make a powerful connection to nature and the universe itself, so if you have a chance to find them in your vicinity, go ahead and sit on them. If not, you can sit on the ground too. Either way, your feet should keep touching the ground. This will allow you to find and maintain a connection with the present.

Casting Circle

Whether an act is performed alone or in a group, most practitioners agree that a sacred circle is one of the most powerful magical tools you can use. Casting circles allows you to create sacred space anywhere you choose. Just like grounding, forming the circle focuses your mind on your intent. Within this circle, you can harness more power and protect yourself from malicious intentions and spirits. This is particularly important when you're in a trance and lose complete focus of your surroundings or the ability to actively defend yourself from bad vibes. To make a casting circle, you will need to:

- Trace the boundaries of the area you want the circle to occupy. You can do this by placing objects around the perimeter. Rocks and crystals work the best, but you can also use any other tools to which you feel drawn.
- Cleanse the space inside the circle. To ensure that only positive energy remains around you, you can cleanse the circle by smudging or banishing negative energy with your words.
- Walk around the perimeter and visualize the borders becoming shrouded in bright light to feel even more secure. You can also hold out your staff in front of you and point it towards the boundaries as you walk clockwise. As the light around you burns, it will also help cleanse the circle.
- You can call on any deity or spiritual guide you want to work with and visualize them entering the circle too.
- Take a few deep breaths, and focus on the magical energy coursing through your body. Feel how it expands with every breath you release, as it falls under the influence of your connection with your guides and the universe.
- When you feel your power connecting with energy emanating from the circle's edges, say, "*My work now begins, and the circle is now cast.*"
- Perform your work and close your circle by walking in the opposite direction.

Entering a Trance

To enter into a trance, you'll need your mind to be detached from your daily preoccupations and open to whatever messages you may receive.

This will allow you to interpret the information correctly and use the wisdom you've received daily. Novice practitioners are advised to practice solitary Seiðr alongside an experienced guide. This means addressing only your own questions and not queries from a group of people.

The best place to try reaching an elevated state of mind is outdoors in nature. For the best effects, go outside just before sunset. Being in the dark will help keep distractions to a minimum. Take your staff with you. Start forming your intention when you leave your home by channeling it into your staff. The intent should be as clear-cut as possible and intensive enough to generate a powerful message. Think about your intention like you would about a pressing question you're entertaining during a conversation with a friend. While the spiritual language is universal, you'll need to ensure they understand you correctly and that you'll be able to understand their response too.

When you reach and prepare your space, take a few deep breaths and start focusing on the intention you've formed. There are several ways to do this, including meditation, rocking back and forth, breathing deeply, reciting poetry, or, most popularly, singing. Choose a method you feel drawn to. You'll know you've reached the elevated state when instead of the stimuli from our world, you suddenly start receiving any that don't belong in your current setting. These may be images, sounds, or anything else your senses may pick up. Don't question the messages you receive until you finish your work.

Chapter 6: Working with the Goddess Freyja

Now that you understand a little more about Seiðr Magic and Norse Shamanism, it's essential to look at it in further detail, especially if you're interested in working with the goddess Freyja.

The goddess Freyja.
Eden, Janine and Jim from New York City, CC BY 2.0 <https://creativecommons.org/licenses/by/2.0>, via Wikimedia Commons: https://commons.wikimedia.org/wiki/File:Freyja_(49560740206).jpg

In this chapter, we'll explore the idea of shamanic journeys in further detail and help you understand some shamanic journeys undertaken by figures from Norse spirituality. However, before you can go further in your shamanic journey and understand how to contact the goddess Freyja, you must first understand who she is.

The Goddess Freyja

In Norse mythology, the goddess Freyja was a member of the Vanir rather than the Aesir. The Vanir were another "tribe" of gods and goddesses in Norse spirituality, with the most prominent (and best-known) "tribe" being the Aesir of Asgard.

However, Freyja was not only a member of the Vanir but also an honorary member of the Aesir. She was the goddess of love, fertility, and beauty. Her family included Njord, her father, and Freyr, her brother.

In some stories, Freyja is married to the obscure god Odr. However, many scholars link Odr to Odin and Freyja herself to Frigg, Odin's wife.

As the goddess of beauty, Freyja was considered the "most glorious" of all the Norse goddesses. She was the mistress and ruler of Fólkvangr, one of the afterlives in Norse mythology.

As the mistress of Fólkvangr, Freyja received half of the souls of all Norse people who died in battle. The other half traveled to Valhalla. However, the major difference between Fólkvangr and Valhalla is that Fólkvangr is also open to women who died a "noble death," while Valhalla was only open to warriors who died in battle.

Because Freyja is the mistress of Fólkvangr, some scholars consider her to be a war goddess as well as the goddess of beauty. In fact, they consider her to be a Valkyrie and perhaps the most prominent Valkyrie of them all.

Some attributes of Freyja noted in existing mythology include:

- She owned the mythical torc/necklace, *Brísingamen*, made of gold. In one story, it was stolen by Loki, who had transformed into a seal to do so.
- Cats were sacred to her, and her chariot was drawn by these animals. Other sacred animals to Freyja included pigs and boars. In fact, she also rode a boar with golden bristles.
- Her mother is unknown. Depending on the source, she may have been a sister of Njord, the giantess/goddess of winter Skadi, or Nerthus, the Norse/Germanic version of Mother Earth.

The most prominent myth that involves Freyja involves the theft of the god Thor's hammer, Mjölnir, by the giant Thrym. After Loki discovers the source of the theft, Thrym agrees to return the hammer to Thor as long as he is permitted to marry Freyja.

In one version of the story, Thor tells Freyja to dress as a bride and go with him to meet Thrym. However, on hearing this, Freyja is incensed and refuses to do so, saying that she would be the "lewdest of women" if she agreed.

So, the gods meet to discuss getting Thor's hammer back. At the end of the discussion, Thor agrees to dress up as and pretend to be Freyja in an effort to fool the giant and win his hammer back - a trick that is, ultimately, successful.

Freyja as the First Völva

Aside from her role in Norse myths, Freyja is also known as the first völva.

Along with her brother and father, Freyja became an honorary member of the Aesir following the end of the Aesir and Vanir wars. Their honorary Aesir status also ensured that there would be no future wars that would break out between the two "tribes" of deities.

Following her transition from Vanaheim to Asgard, Freyja taught the Aesir the art of Seiðr Magic. She was the first of the Norse shamans, even before Odin, and in her role as the völva of Asgard and Vahaeim, she was venerated by mortal völvas.

There is evidence that a völva buried around 1000 BC was buried with a silver pendant with a figure that likely represented Freyja wearing her torc Brísingamen.

As a practitioner of Seiðr Magic, Freyja understood the workings of fate and how to use that understanding to change fate. In some accounts, Freyja is considered to be greedy and evil for teaching the other gods how to perform Seiðr Magic.

However, Seiðr Magic is a twofold ability. While it can be used to create negative consequences for the victim of a practitioner, it can also be used to bring about positive change. While, in some stories, the ability to wield Seiðr Magic is considered to be evil, it is more commonly a neutral ability whose direction is dictated by the user.

There are hints throughout Norse myths of the power that Freyja was able to wield as the first practitioner of Seiðr Magic. For example, in one story, Freyja is able to transform into a falcon with the help of falcon feathers that she owns. She can also lend these feathers (in some stories, these are not individual feathers, rather, they are part of a cloak of feathers) to allow them to change their shape. For example, she lends these feathers/cloak to Loki to help him discover the culprit behind the theft of Thor's hammer, Mjölnir.

Additionally, there is also the role of Freyja as the wife of Odr.

In one of the few stories that survive about the god Odr, he travels away from the other gods. Where and why he goes has not survived – only the fact that he leaves. Freyja, who loves her husband, searches for him but cannot find him. In her anguish, she cries tears of gold as she continues her search.

For some scholars, Freyja's search for Odr represents an early version of the shamanic journey. Additionally, as Odr is associated with Odin (and Freyja with Frigg), there is a possibility that this tale represents a story where Freyja/Frigg go in search of Odr/Odin during the period when Odin goes on his own shamanic journey, hanging himself from a branch of Yggdrasil as part of his discovery of runes.

Additionally, stories say that Odin traveled extensively to distant lands. This may, once again, be why Freyja/Frigg was called to travel in search of Odr/Odin, going on her own shamanic journey parallel to her husband's.

Freyja's Powers in Relation to Other Deities

It's essential to note that while Freyja was the first völva, she was not the most powerful.

That honor rested with the Norns.

The Norns were generally represented by a group of three women who wove the fate of mortals and gods. Even Odin was forced to consult with the Norns when he wanted to discern his own future.

As the weavers of fate, the Norns were the most powerful völvas and the most powerful wielders of Seiðr Magic.

Understanding the Shamanic Journey

It is essential to note that in Norse Shamanism, the journey taken by the völva was different from the shamanic journey.

Völvas were generally women. Norse shamans, on the other hand, were both men and women, and this distinction meant that rituals between völvas and shamans differed.

The major known ritual of a völva is that of the prophecy.

Völvas were traveling women who traveled from community to community, likely with a group of young women. She would visit a community when called to help with prophesying important information, such as when a famine would end or when the rain would arrive.

After arriving at a community, the völva would take the time to understand the community and its environment. After that, she would be fed a feast of animal hearts. The hearts would come from as many different types of animals as could be found in the environment.

It is possible that the animals killed for the völva's feast were part of a ritual sacrifice, the information about which has not survived. Additionally, others likely ate the meat from the animals killed for the feast, possibly the women she traveled with or community members.

After eating her feast, it was time for the völva to make a prophecy.

As part of the prophecy ritual, the völva was seated on a special cushion that was made with hen feathers. Following this, a special song was sung to enable her to enter a prophesied trance. The song helped summon spirits, which the völva would use to make her prophecy.

She would use the information imparted to her by the spirits to answer the question(s) posed to her by the community. Most commonly, the völva was summoned to help prophecy the end of famines. If left unchecked, they could devastate communities and kill scores of people.

That said, this was a ritual used only by the völvas. For the Norse shamans, the shamanic journey involved other steps that resembled the ones Odin took during his shamanic journey to find and reveal the knowledge of runes.

As part of the shamanic journey, purification was carried out using sacred herbs. The herbs were used to eliminate distractions that might draw the shaman's attention away from the journey they were undertaking.

The space to be purified would be determined by the leader of the group of shamans – generally, the person who would be undertaking the journey. The process of going on a shamanic journey as part of Norse Shamanism and the practice of Seiðr Magic was not a solo one. Rather, it was performed by a group of participants.

Once the space where the journey was to take place was purified, the next step was to call on the directions, the nature spirits, and the gods.

When calling on the gods, special attention was paid to the deities associated with Seiðr Magic, such as Odin, Freyja, and the Norns.

It should be noted that this procedure was not necessary for taking a shamanic journey, and it is possible to go through a journey without undergoing this level of ritual. However, these ritual steps ensure that everyone involved in the journey is fully involved in the process and is not distracted by other concerns. In essence, it served a psychological purpose rather than a practical one.

Once the area was prepared, the journey started with ritual words. After the ritual words were spoken, the participants began drumming, chanting, and singing. The energy created by doing this was transferred to the shaman, who could then use it as part of their journey.

One member of the participants (generally the drummer) acted as a guide, helping the shaman on their journey. The drum beat helped determine how the shaman proceeded on their journey, and the guide also provided instructions on what the shaman should do.

As the journey started, the shaman would relax their body, breathe deeply, and start visualizing their journey. The mental journey would take place in the Sacred Grove, which formed the gateway between the mortal and spirit worlds. The Sacred Grove is the home of Yggdrasil, the World Tree.

From the Sacred Grove, the shaman travels down Yggdrasil to the Underworld/Hel. They do not enter the Underworld immediately, not being dead themselves; rather, they stand before the Gate of the Underworld, asking their questions and letting the spirits answer them.

While the shaman undertakes their spiritual journey, the guide continues to narrate it to the other participants. This way, all the people participating are able to vicariously experience the shaman's journey.

Once the other participants have completed their own symbolic journeys and arrive at the Gate to the Underworld with the shaman, he can enter the Underworld. This is the second part of the ritual, the part that only the shaman will undertake.

Once the shaman enters the Underworld, their experience is unique to each person. Some shamans will ask questions out loud, others will visualize them, and so on.

After the shaman has the answers they were looking for, the guide will signal the start of the end of the journey. At this point, the observers will ask their questions verbally to the shaman. Questions must be as simple and specific as possible to allow the shaman to provide a specific answer.

The guide also keeps an eye on the shaman, helping to end the question session if they notice fatigue. As part of the questioning session, the shaman may also channel the spirits of the dead, although this depends entirely on the spirits and the questions asked of them.

Once the questions have been answered or the shaman tires, the guide helps him make the journey back to the mortal world. If more questions are answered, the process may be repeated for a second shaman, then a third, and so on. This depends on the number of questions to be asked and the number of shamans present.

As the last one makes the journey back home, the guide narrates the return journey as they make the journey to the Underworld. This allows the observers to return from their own journeys and signals an end to the ritual of the shamanic journey. Once the journey is over, the observers, shaman, and guide must all eat and drink to replenish their energy.

Journeying to Freyja

As modern Seiðr Magic practitioners, your first shamanic journey should be to meet Freyja. Not only is she the First Völva as the teacher of Seiðr Magic, but she is also the First Shaman.

As part of your shamanic journey to meet Freyja, you must first meditate on her to connect with her before you can attempt a proper shamanic journey.

To meditate on Freyja, you should:

- Choose an essential oil blend that you like or that aligns with Freyja. Some options you can consider include lemon verbena, geranium, lime, and jasmine.
- Apply some of the oil to the palm of your hand. The left hand is the better option, though you can use your right hand as well, depending on what you're most comfortable with.
- Inhale the scent of the essential oil to begin your meditation.
- Close your eyes and let your worries fall away. Once you're relaxed, call on your guide and guardians, as well as the spirits of the four directions and elements, to help guide you during your meditation.

- Put forth your intention with this meditation – to connect with the goddess Freyja, the first shaman. Put forth these intentions to Nerthus, a potential mother of Freyja and the representation of Mother Earth.
- Call upon the goddess Freyja, thanking her for her presence. Give yourself the space to connect with her consciousness, allowing yourself to bask in her presence and appreciate her dual roles at the First Völva and First Shaman.
- Once you're done with your meditation, thank the spirits who have helped you connect with Freyja and let go of the energy you're holding on to.

Once you've connected with Freyja, you can then start practicing for your shamanic journey. Remember, you will need someone to act as a guide, so you must choose your companion carefully.

Now that you understand how to connect with Freyja and practice to undertake a shamanic journey, the next step is to understand how to travel through Yggdrasil during this journey.

Chapter 7: Journeying through Yggdrasill

A sacred giant living ash tree that holds the universe together and lies at its heart. Deities and humans have been drawn to the World Tree, Yggdrasill, since time immemorial. Because everything leads back to Yggdrasil, the tree holds great spiritual value to many. It is easily the most important entity in Norse traditions.

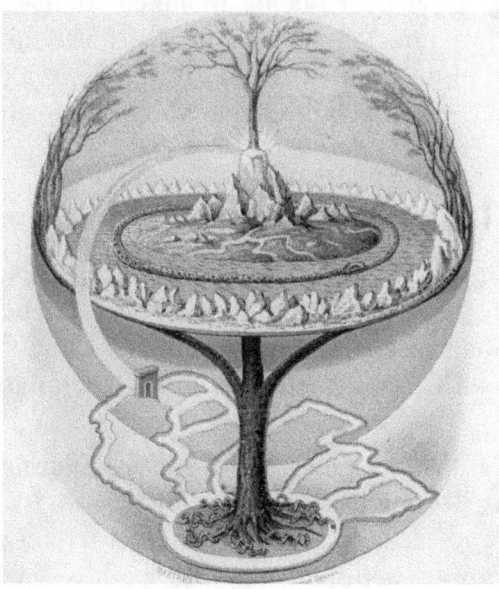

Because everything leads back to Yggdrasil, the tree holds great spiritual value to many.
https://commons.wikimedia.org/wiki/File:Yggdrasil.jpg

Being the root of the entire universe, the majestic tree holds the answers to many questions. That's what the deities and wise men that once roamed the Earth thought. Following their footsteps, you can also attempt to unravel the tree's power and mystery and walk among the gods.

Before you do that, take this opportunity to contemplate the magnificence of Yggdrasill and its significance to the cosmos. This chapter will explore that and guide you through a wonderful journey through the realms surrounding Yggdrasil.

The Story behind Yggdrasill

The closest thing to Yggdrasill in other religions and mythologies is the Tree of Life concept. Trees are sacred in countless beliefs and are seen as symbols of life, rebirth, knowledge, and the cyclical nature of the universe, among other things.

While Yggdrasill represents similar concepts, it also supports the entire universe and is a sacred place to both deities and humans. The gods would assemble at its base every day and watch over the realms. Many kinds of creatures lurk in several parts of the tree.

How Yggdrasill came into existence is not known. It may have always existed, but several things suggest that it is mortal, which we'll cover later on. Naturally, Yggdrasill's well-being is linked to that of the universe. What we do know, however, is that it is a powerful symbol and an accurate depiction of the cycle of nature. It may be in a different plane of existence altogether, but it possesses incredible energy that draws in both gods and humans.

The Center of the Cosmos

The universe comprises nine realms, all spread out from Yggdrasil's branches and roots and occupying different levels. The tree's branches stretch far above the heavens. Yggdrasill is referred to as "the friend of the clear sky" in the old Völuspá poem. The roots reach into the underworld realms.

Because Yggdrasil is the center of the universe, journeying through the realms takes place through it. The way the world is arranged around Yggdrasil is not always clear, but the tree definitely connects all parts of the world. We'll cover the realms surrounding Yggdrasil in more detail later on.

The Tree of Wisdom: Odin's Sacrifices

Besides being the very center of the universe, Yggdrasil is associated with wisdom and knowledge. Odin was absolutely relentless in his pursuit of knowledge. For a long time, he observed the well of Urd from which Yggdrasill grows. He saw that Mimir, who had unparalleled wisdom, often drank from the well. Seeking enlightenment and wisdom, Odin set out to drink from the well but had to sacrifice an eye in return, which he did.

The well is home to powerful creatures known as the Norns, who created and controlled the fates of all beings, including gods. They did this by carving runes that were then carried throughout Yggdrasill. Determined to figure out the secret behind the runes, Odin pierced himself with a spear, hung himself from one of the tree's branches, and kept staring down at the well for nine days until the runes finally revealed themselves to him.

Because of Odin's divine sacrifice, Yggdrasill is seen as a source of cosmic knowledge, wisdom, and enlightenment.

Ragnarök: A New Beginning

The fate of Yggdrasill and the universe are intertwined. While Yggdrasill has always existed, it is not immortal, and its downfall may signal the universe's destruction. Its mortality is perhaps symbolized by the four stags continually feeding from it and bringing it closer to decay. Therefore, the tree needs compassion and protection to nourish life.

Yggdrasill plays a crucial role in the events of Ragnarök, but its fate remains unclear. Come Ragnarök, there will be chaos all around. The sky will split, the stars will disappear, the realms will be destroyed, and Yggdrasill will tremble. Most gods, demons, giants, and humans will die in Ragnarök.

Yggdrasill will quaver and will seem to fall and end life as we know it, particularly when Surtr, the fire giant, flings his fire and almost ravages it to the ground. However, it will endure and signal a new beginning for humankind. Yggdrasill's trunk will provide shelter for the surviving gods as well as the two last humans, Líf and Lífþrasir. From there, a new universe will emerge, and life will continue in a world free of chaos.

The World around Yggdrasill

Yggdrasill stands in the very middle of the Norse universe and is the bridge connecting all parts of the world.

The Nine Realms

Yggdrasill is the cosmic tree that extends to the farthest reaches of the universe and holds the nine realms within its roots and branches.

1. **Asgard:** Home to the Æsir gods and goddesses, Asgard is where the gates to the great halls of Valhalla are located. This realm is believed to be high up in the sky and connected to the realm of humankind via a rainbow bridge.

2. **Vanaheim:** Just as the Æsir settled in Asgard, the Vanir deities established their home in Vanaheim. While there is no clear description of what the Vanaheim is like, it is probably a magical and fertile realm since the Vanir are associated with sorcery, magic, and nature.

3. **Alfheim::** Ruled by the Vanir God Freyr, Alfheim is the homeland of the Ljósálfar, light elves who were described as "fairer than the sun to look at" in the Prose Edda. The light elves are considered patrons of art, poetry, and music. Alfheim is thought to be located in the heavens along with Asgard and Vanaheim.

4. **Jotunheim:** The sworn enemies of the Æsir gods are the Jötnar, or giants, who inhabit the chaotic realm of Jotunheim. The realm is thought to be separated from Asgard by the eternally flowing river of Ífingr that is almost impossible to cross. One of Yggdrasil's great roots extends to Mimir's well, located in Jotunheim.

5. **Midgard:** The home of humankind, this lies in the middle of the world and around Yggdrasill. Surrounding Midgard is a vast impassable ocean guarded by the World Serpent Jörmungandr, child of Loki and the giantess Angrboða. Midgard was fashioned by Odin and his brothers Vili and Vé from the body parts of the giant Augelmir, the ancestor of all Jötnar and the very first being in the universe.

6. **Svartalfheim/Nidavellir:** This cold, dark realm is the home of the dwarves, known for their immense magic and craftsmanship abilities. This is where Mjölnir, Thor's infamous hammer, was

forged. Odin's magical golden ring, Draupnir, and his spear, Gungnir, were also crafted by the dwarves in Nidavellir.

7. **Muspelheim:** Back when nothing else but Yggdrasil and the void of Ginnungagap existed, the fire realm Muspelheim and the dark, icy, misty realm Niflheim were the first to come into existence. Muspelheim is home to the fire giants, led by Surtr, the arch nemesis of the Æsir.

8. **Niflheim:** On the opposite side of the universe from Muspelheim lies the primordial land of fog and mist known as Niflheim. The dark, cold realm is home to the eleven freezing-cold rivers of Élivágar, stemming from the wellspring Hvergelmir. One of Yggdrasill's roots extends all the way to Hvergelmir. Niflheim, along with Muspelheim, is seen as the origin of all living beings. The giant Ymir, who is the first being in the universe, was created when the ice of Niflheim mixed with the fire of Muspelheim.

9. **Hel:** Ruled over by the goddess or giantess Hel, another child of Loki and Angrboða, Hel is the Norse underworld where all those unworthy of Valhalla are cast. Hel's location sometimes overlaps with that of Niflheim. Hel is also said to be beneath the root of Yggdrasill that extends to Hvergelmir. However, the two realms are described very differently in Norse mythology.

The link between Yggdrasill and the nine realms is undeniable and acts as a powerful symbol, that is, the interconnectivity of all the universe's elements. With that in mind, how the various worlds are arranged around Yggdrasill is difficult to decide. For instance, little is known about some of the realms and how they can be reached. Journeying through the realms was reserved only for the most intrepid of travelers, gods or otherwise. Several paths separating realms are well-known. Even those are impossible to cross, except for a very few beings.

Several attempts have been made to reconstruct Norse cosmology. The realms are thought by many to spread out from the branches of Yggdrasill. Consequently, they will lie on different levels. Based on this view of the Norse universe, the realms of Asgard, Vanaheim, and Alfheim occupy the highest level and constitute the heavens. Midgard is in the middle, and along with it are Jotunheim and Nidavellir. The lowest level represents the underworld and includes Muspelheim, Niflheim, and Helheim. Yggdrasill has three great roots extending to Jotunheim, up towards Asgard, and down to Niflheim.

Another approach acknowledges these 3 levels but suggests that the realms are all beneath Yggdrasill. Similarly, Yggdrasill's roots extend to each level, reaching Asgard, Jotunheim, and Niflheim.

The Creatures of Yggdrasill

A variety of fantastic beasts lurk in and around Yggdrasill. At the very top of the tree sits an unnamed eagle and a hawk known as Veðrfölnir. Underneath the lowermost root in Niflheim is a monstrous serpent named Níðhöggr, who continuously eats away at the root. A squirrel named Ratatoskr runs up and down Yggdrasill and carries messages between the eagle and the serpent. Four stags named Dvalinn, Dáinn, Duneyrr, and Duraþrór move around the tree branches and nibble on its leaves, while the Norns of the Well of Urdr in Asgard (the well holds one of Yggdrasill's roots) keep healing and nourishing the tree. In the ocean surrounding Midgard lurks the World Serpent Jörmungandr, often depicted as circling around Yggdrasill.

The Wells of Yggdrasill

Yggdrasill is watered by three sacred wells that play a significant role in Norse mythology. Each well is located in a path connecting Yggdrasill and a specific realm.

Urðarbrunnr, or the Well of Urðr

The fate of all creation is decided by the Norns that inhabit the well of Urdr. It is located beneath Yggdrasill's root in Asgard and where the gods are thought to assemble daily. The Well of Urdr is the setting of Odin's ultimate sacrifice that led him to unravel the secret behind the runes.

Mímisbrunn, or Mimir's Well

One of the three Yggdrasill's roots extends to Mimir's well, located in the realm of the giants, Jotunheim. As the name suggests, the well is guarded by Mimir, a figure with immense knowledge and wisdom achieved by drinking from the well. Mimir's well is the central element of Odin's eye sacrifice mentioned earlier in the chapter.

Hvergelmir

Yggdrasill's third great root extends all the way down to Niflheim, precisely at the Hvergelmir. The wellspring is the first source of water that came into existence and is a crucial element in the creation of the very first being, the giant Ymir. Hvergelmir is home to a large number of snakes as well as the serpent Níðhöggr, who keeps gnawing at the root of Yggdrasill.

Your First Journey through Yggdrasill

By now, you're familiar with the significance of Yggdrasill and can set the scene for a journey of self-discovery and enlightenment. Following the footsteps of Odin, the epitome of spiritual journeying, you can also aim to attain higher consciousness and spiritual awareness through Yggdrasill and its surrounding realms.

Yggdrasill houses all aspects of life and consciousness. It encompasses powerful energy and is shrouded in mystery that does not unravel easily, not even for the likes of Odin. Such a journey requires a great deal of curiosity, devotion, and patience.

Balancing Your Energies

Before your cosmic journey, you must be well-prepared physically and mentally. This can be achieved by various meditative practices, both old and new. The aim is to balance your inner energies and clear your mind of all distractions, making it easier to channel the right energy for your journey.

An efficient practice to attain a state of relaxation is through grounding, a traditional Norse Magic practice, which you can perform in honor of Jörð, the mother of Thor and the personification of Earth. The best way to ground yourself to Jörd would be outdoors in nature, ideally with your bare feet touching the ground.

Close your eyes and visualize your distractions being pushed down through your body to your feet and into the ground. Take slow deep breaths in the process, as this will help you cleanse your mind faster. Afterward, visualize drawing the Earth's vital energy to your body. Stay as relaxed and focused as you can, and let Jörd's energy flow through every part of your body. By the time you're done, you should feel refreshed and transformed, which will aid you in your journey.

Interpreting Yggdrasill and the Nine Realms

Depictions of Yggdrasill and the Norse universe are plenty. You can make your journey far more illustrious through the power of imagery. One of the best ways to enhance your journey is by setting up an indoor or outdoor altar. To represent Yggdrasill, you can use tree branches and leaves, preferably from evergreens like ash. A drawing or a model of

Yggdrasill also works.

Around your representation of the tree, consider lighting candles, especially if you're inside your home. In Norse traditions, candles are powerful ritual elements and can help you work better with spirits to ease your journey. Upon learning about each realm and its figures and symbols, you can associate each realm with a specific color and choose your candle colors accordingly.

You can also place offerings of rocks, crystals, runes, and herbs with medicinal and magical properties around the altar. Your altar will help you visualize your journey and know what you're looking for. Keep in mind that your journey will be unique, and so should your altar.

Opening the Doors of Perception

Your voyage through Yggdrasill and its nine realms is a path toward an elevated state of consciousness. By creating a suitable setting, you can enter an ecstatic trance that can open your mind to wonderful revelations about yourself and the world around you. Several things can enhance your state of trance.

Drumming Journey

Drums are used in many Norse rituals and are known to have various uses, including healing, ceremonies, journeying between worlds, and invoking spirits. The rhythmic beat of Shamanic journey drums has a powerful effect and can help alter your perception and increase the likelihood of communing with helping spirits.

Runic Chanting

Chanting the runes is a powerful traditional Norse ritual and is a crucial element in Galdr magic, which we'll cover in more detail in a later chapter. It is a powerful spell incantation that helps you enter a state of trance. You can focus on a few runes at a time and chant their names, preferably along the shamanic drum beats. For this purpose, you should familiarize yourself with the meaning and symbolism of runes to help you choose the runes to be chanted.

Runes are important elements that allude to Odin's divine sacrifice in Yggdrasill. There are no wrong ways to choose your runes as long as they are of significance to you. While chanting the runes, it's important to visualize or reflect on their meaning. Runes are a great source of insight and can be a recurring image in your journey.

Making Your Path

By now, you're likely to notice changes in your perception and find yourself completely focused and immersed in your experience. Even then, you can still use the help of spiritual guides that you can call at any time. Spirits are often of great help to those who reach out to them. As long as your intentions are clear and well-formulated, you can allow yourself to be guided by spirits. The practice of Seiðr can be very useful at this stage.

Your journey through Yggdrasill should be one of ascension and transformation. Try to visualize yourself at the root that extends all the way down to Hvergelmir in Niflheim. Acknowledge and embrace the darkness of the underworld realms and the vile creatures that nibble away at Yggdrasill. After reflecting on that, you can make your way up to the middle realms where giants, dwarves, and humans dwell. These realms represent our everyday perception of reality and are crucial in understanding who we are and our place in the universe. From there, carve your path toward the heavenly realms that exist on the highest plane of consciousness in the universe.

Make sure to spend as much time as possible exploring, contemplating, and honoring the experience. Don't hesitate to ask your helping spirits for guidance and stay connected to them for as long as the journey takes. Whichever path you've been taken into, embrace it and come out as a transformed being. Put the insights you gain to good use in your everyday life.

Chapter 8: Norse Runes 101

This chapter discusses the origins of the runes and how they were used in ancient times. After reading it, you'll learn their English and phonetic equivalents and their meanings. While runes as an alphabet aren't used in modern languages, you'll receive plenty of advice on how to use them to write modern texts, starting with a few simple words and sentences. Just like runic meditation, this will help you familiarize yourself with the shape and energy of the runes. This knowledge will come in handy in runic divination and similar rune magic practices.

The Origins of the Runes

According to Norse lore, the runes were revealed to people by the deities. The first who came upon them was Odin after he hung from the Yggdrasil, the World Tree, for 9 days and nights without food, water, or sleep. After learning about their magical power, Odin decided to share the runes with everyone else, allowing their wisdom to be harnessed for different purposes. Runic inscriptions were found on the belongings of Germanic tribes that lived around 50 CE.

The earliest known record of the first complete set of runes dates to around 400. This was the first runic alphabet, known as "Futhark" by the Norse. The name of the alphabet is derived from its first letters. These were Fehu, Uruz, Thurisaz, Ansuz, Raidho, and Kenaz. This first runic alphabet was called Elder Futhark and was used until the 8th century. It consisted of 24 runes, divided into three aettir, the groups ruled over by prominent Norse deities. The first runes of each ættir (Fehu, Hagalaz, and

Tiwaz) are also called the Mother Runes because they were believed to be the first additions to the Elder Futhark. In addition, the other runes in their respective groups can be tied to them phonetically. This is evidence of how the entire alphabet was used as a phonetic system rather than a written form of the spoken Norse language.

In Scandinavia, the Elder Futhark was shortened to 16 runes, becoming the Younger Futhark. Unlike its predecessor, this alphabet was easier to use. The runes were less complex, and there weren't any harsh lines involved in their carving. In other parts of Europe, the Elder Futhark changed into Anglo-Saxon Futhorc (used until the 11th century) and later the Medieval Futhark (used from the 12th to the 15th century).

How Runes Were Used in Ancient Times

Both written and oral records confirm that the ancient Germanic tribes used the runes for several purposes. For starters, the runes were their written form of communication. The most educated members of the tribes recorded each significant event by carving the runes and inscribing them into stone or wood. At first, runes were carved into massive stone monuments, testifying to the tribe's achievements. Later, they became smaller objects, which the people could take with them as they traveled. They also started to incorporate runes into art and clothes manufacturing and were then taken over by the followers of other religions.

Besides a writing tool, the runes were also used for magical practices. They were into folk magic work with Celtic origins, such as divination and spiritual communication. They are believed to be infused with natural magic. Each carries a slightly different spiritual substance. Due to their magical essence, runes could foster communication between all that's encompassed by the universal spirit. They could also take on a person or being's own magic, which allowed for more efficient communication.

As knowledge of the runes began to spread among the population, there was confusion about their use. Those who only had a rudimentary understanding of their magical side often used runes for the wrong purposes, causing more harm than good, even if this wasn't their intention.

The Meaning of the Elder Futhark Runes

The runes in the Elder Futhark alphabet have several meanings. Most of these are tied to natural forces. These can change and evolve with time, just as nature does through each cycle. Consequently, the interpretation of each rune depends on how it's affected by these changes at any given time. That said, several runic correspondences are just as relevant as they were in ancient times. Here is what each rune in the Elder Futhark alphabet means in modern English, alongside their phonetic equivalent and modern pronunciation.

Freyr's Aett

As the son of the sea God Njörd, Freyr is one of the most prominent deities of the Norse pantheon. He is the god of fertility, peace, and new beginnings. The runes in his aett represent creativity, finding your way to establish material security and the early stages of spiritual development.

ᚠ - Fehu

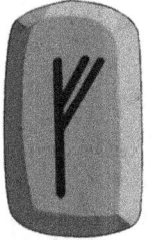

Fehu.
https://pixabay.com/es/illustrations/fehu-runa-fe-runa-adivinaci%c3%b3n-6508602/

Modern phoneme: F

English pronunciation: "FAY-hoo"

Fehu, in English, means cattle or wealth. However, it can also illustrate the realization of dreams and significant goals, good luck, material gain, and property, not to mention hope for improving one's life.

ᚢ - Uruz

Uruz.
https://pixabay.com/es/illustrations/uruz-ur-runa-futhark-n%c3%b3rdico-6508604/

Modern phoneme: U
English pronunciation: "OO-rooz"

Uruz is translated as "bull" or "wild ox." Representing the power of this animal, this rune is linked to perseverance, endurance, willpower, physical health, and vitality. It also reveals more goals to be achieved and challenges to be overcome through courageous behavior.

Þ - Thurisaz

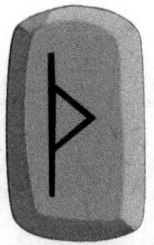

Thurisaz.
https://pixabay.com/es/illustrations/thurisaz-jueves-runa-futhark-6508603/

Modern phoneme: Th
English pronunciation: "THUR-ee-sazh"

This rune is translated as "giant" or "thorn" in English. It's also the universal Norse symbol for the hammer of Thor. Like the hammer, the rune illustrates protection and defense. At the same time, it can point to danger, disruptive forces, or conflict. Thurisaz means purification, and cathartic forces bring divine wisdom.

ᚠ - Ansuz

Ansuz.
https://pixabay.com/es/illustrations/ansuz-runa-runas-futhark-2644294/

Modern phoneme: A

English Pronunciation: "AHN-sooz"

The meaning of Ansuz is revelation or message. It is linked to several Norse deities, including Odin, the master of communication. The rune indicates messages and insight one may receive through visions and signs. It also represents everything that has to do with oral communication, including the mouth and the vocal cords.

R - Raidho

Raidho.
https://pixabay.com/es/illustrations/raidho-runa-runas-futhark-2644605/

Modern phoneme: R

English pronunciation: "Rah-EED-ho"

The literal meaning of this rune is "traveling on horseback" or simply "journey." In broad terms, Raidho can also represent any form of movement or progress in life, including finding new perspectives and spiritual growth. It may also refer to intuitively channeling your energy, working on goals, and making better decisions.

ᚲ - Kenaz

Kenaz.
https://pixabay.com/es/illustrations/kenaz-runa-runas-futhark-2644856/

Modern phoneme: C / K

English pronunciation: "KEN-ahz"

Kenaz has a general meaning in the old Norse language. One is "ulcer," which is linked to gut feelings, passion, and following your dreams. The other meaning of the rune is the "torch," the symbol of enlightenment and transformation. It's believed to illuminate one's purpose or the need to follow your dreams regardless of outside influences.

X - Gebo

Gebo.
https://pixabay.com/es/illustrations/gebo-runa-runas-futhark-2644831/

Modern phoneme: G

English pronunciation: "GHEB-o"

In English, Gebo means "gift." However, this rune can also represent service, assistance, luck, or even partnerships you can obtain by providing the same. Gebo also illustrates the need for charity, generosity, and the exchange of equal-value properties. The appearance of the rune is also viewed as a sign of thankfulness.

ᚹ - Wunjo

Wunjo.
https://pixabay.com/es/illustrations/wunjo-runa-runas-futhark-2644556/

Modern phoneme: W

English pronunciation: "WOON-yo"

This rune represents joy, well-being, and happiness. However, Wunjo often signifies distress and challenges that predate the fulfillment of one's dreams. It can also signal impending changes and unexpected losses.

Heimdall's Aett

Heimdall is another powerful figure in Norse mythology. He is the gatekeeper and teacher of the deities. He is also the one who watches over the wisdom distributed by the gods. The runes of his aett lead the way to growth and prosperity. This is often obtained through a journey that contains both losses and successes.

ᚺ - Hagalaz

Hagalaz.
https://pixabay.com/es/illustrations/hagalaz-runa-runas-futhark-2644694/

Modern phoneme: H

English pronunciation: "HA-ga-lah"

Hagalaz means "hail" in English. This rune illustrates delay and difficulty releasing plans and the signal for change that's needed to move forward with your life. It's also linked to natural disasters and their consequences or unclear forces.

ᚾ - Naudhiz

Modern phoneme: N

English pronunciation: "NOWD-heez"

Naudhiz is the rune representing need in general. However, it may also signify difficulties, distress, the lack of a crucial quality, and resistance to change. The rune may also show that you will overcome life's hurdles by manifesting your wishes through intuitive practices.

I - Isa

Isa.

https://pixabay.com/es/illustrations/isa-runa-runas-futhark-adivinaci%c3%b3n-2644662/

Modern phoneme: I

English pronunciation: "EE-sa"

This rune signifies "ice," or being frozen in time, which means waiting. It also represents stillness, inertia, and the period of calm before taking action. It often appears as a period before a significant change, such as switching the course of your life, opening to a new perspective, etc.

ᛃ - Jera

Jera.
https://pixabay.com/es/illustrations/jera-runa-runas-futhark-2644821/

Modern phoneme: J / Y

English pronunciation: "YARL-a"

Jera, or "year" in English, is the old Norse symbol for harvest. However, the rune also means reaping your rewards for hard work or a successful conclusion of a difficult period. Jera can also showcase the beginning of a new life period cycle, the opportunity to grow and gather wisdom.

ᛇ - Eihwaz

Eihwaz.
https://pixabay.com/es/illustrations/eihwaz-runa-runas-futhark-2644633/

Modern phoneme: E / I
English pronunciation: "AY-wahz"

In the English language, this rune means "yew." In Norse lore, the yew tree symbolizes mystery and inspiration. It is believed to represent the stability and grounding needed to find spiritual wisdom. The rune can also show the sacrifices you need to make to thrive.

ᛈ - Perthro

Perthro.
https://pixabay.com/es/illustrations/perthro-runa-runas-futhark-2644941/

Modern phoneme: P
English pronunciation: "PER-thro"

Perthro is the symbol that represents fate and prophecy, although it's also linked to mysticism and the occult. It may reveal the correlation between present action and future outcomes. It can also mean industriousness, awareness, and fertility in different aspects of life.

ᛉ - Algiz

Modern phoneme: Z
English pronunciation: "AL-geez"

This rune means "elk" in English. This animal is known for its courage and protective nature. Consequently, the rune illustrates the need to listen to your creative instincts and their ability to bring enlightenment, good luck, and spiritual wisdom.

ᛋ - Sowilo

Sowilo.
https://pixabay.com/es/illustrations/sowilo-runa-runas-futhark-2644331/

Modern phoneme: S

English pronunciation: "So-WEE-lo"

Sowilo is the symbol of "sun" and happiness. Like its namesake, the rune also represents vitality, abundance in nourishment, and perseverance against challenges. Sowilo may also illuminate the path to finding solace, motivation, and true happiness in life.

Tyr's Aett

Tyr, the Norse deity ruling the skies, is also the symbol of war and justice. The runes in his aett refer to both physical and spiritual development. They also indicate that if you can focus on overcoming life's challenges, you'll be able to create a life of which you're proud.

↑ - Tiwaz

Modern phoneme: T

English pronunciation: "TEE-wahz"

The first rule in this aett is the most common symbol of "the god Thor." It symbolizes all the qualities he is feared and honored for, including strength, bravery, leadership, and honor. Tiwaz also appears to signify the greater good and sacrifices that lead to success.

ᛒ - Berkano

Berkano.
https://pixabay.com/es/illustrations/berkana-runa-runas-futhark-2644529/

Modern phoneme: B

English pronunciation: "BER-Kah-no"

Berkano is the Norse symbol for the birch tree, but it is also associated with the birch goddess. It represents the beginning of something new, rebirth, a period of fertility. It often appears in relationships, whether to signal to begin anew or to grow into something more powerful.

ᛖ - Ehwaz

Ehwaz.
https://pixabay.com/es/illustrations/ehwaz-runa-runas-futhark-2644896/

Modern phoneme: E

English pronunciation: "EH-wahz"

This rune means "horse" in modern English. As the Norse warriors' loyal companion, the horse is the ancient symbol of trust and partnership between different beings. It can also indicate fate in your success, instinctive behavior, and assistance.

ᛗ - Mannaz

Mannaz.
https://pixabay.com/es/illustrations/mannaz-runa-runas-futhark-2644241/

Modern phoneme: M

English pronunciation: "MAN-Naz"

Mannaz is the rune for the English word "man." It represents humanity and its qualities like mortality or going through the stages of life and death and forming communities where different values and skills can be developed.

ᛚ - Laguz

Laguz.
https://pixabay.com/es/illustrations/laguz-runa-runas-futhark-2644773/

Modern phoneme: L

English pronunciation: "LAH-gooz"

The meaning of this rune is tied to water, the unknown, potentials, the fluidity of emotions, and inner awareness of them. It also symbolizes open-mindedness, dreams, imagination, and emotional healing.

◊ - Ingwaz

Modern phoneme: Ng

English pronunciation: "ING-wahz"

This rune is linked to the god of Ingwaz. Like this deity, the rune presents sexuality, fresh energy, ancestors, family, wisdom accumulated over time, and spiritual growth. It also symbolizes a period of inner peace.

⏣ - Othala

Othala.
https://pixabay.com/es/illustrations/othala-runa-runas-futhark-2644445/

Modern phoneme: O

English pronunciation: "OH-tha-la"

In English, this rune means "inheritance" or "tradition." Othala is linked to wisdom, property, and value that represent your legacy, the one you inherited from Others themselves. It can also represent homecoming, heritage, nobility, and talents.

ᛗ - Dagaz

Dagaz.
https://pixabay.com/es/illustrations/dagaz-runa-runas-futhark-2644493/

Modern phoneme: D
English pronunciation: "DAH-gahz"

Dagaz is a Norse word for "day." Just like a new day, this rune carries the meaning of hope, inspiration, awakening, and much-needed changes. It can also represent harmony, spiritual growth, clarity, self-awareness, and the ultimate happiness that comes with the realization of your dreams.

Runes in Practice

Besides magic, you can also use runes to translate short texts from English to Norse. For example, you can write your name or a simple phrase. It's a good idea to start with your name, as there are a few rules to writing in runes. Study the English equivalents of the runes from above before you start writing anything. Write them out on paper in the form of a table, so you'll have a reference anytime you need to look up a letter.

Remember to pen down the letters as you pronounce them. For example, if your name is Christina, you'll need to write "Kristina" in runes. In practice, this would look like this: ᚲᚱᛁᛋᛏᛁᚾᚨ.

Another rule of thumb is if you have a letter duplication in your name or the phrase you're trying to translate, these won't be duplicated in the Futhark. For instance, if your name is Emma, you'll write this as "Ema" in Futhark. In runes, this would look like this: ᛖᛗᚨ. The same rule applies if two consecutive letters correspond to the same rune. Let's say your name is Jack. The Kenaz rune corresponds to the letters "C" and "K," which means you'll have it twice in your name. However, you'll only write it once: ᛋᚠᚲ.

After writing down your first name, you can try to write your full name, including all last and middle names. When you're confident enough to write your full name correctly, you can move on to writing simple sentences. When you're writing more than one word or sentence, you can decide whether to leave a space between them or not. Some chose to use a dot (·) to separate the words, which is an easy way to ensure you're leaving enough space between the words. It also helps us remember which world each rule belongs to. Here are a few sentences to help you practice:

Today is a sunny day. ᛏᛟᛞᚨᛋ·ᛁᛋ·ᚠ·ᛋᚢᛏᛋ·ᛞᚨᛋ

The cat is chasing its tail. ᚦᛗ·ᚲᚠᛏ·ᛁᛋ·ᚲᚺᚠᛋᛁᚷ·ᛁᛏᛋ·ᛏᚠᛁᛚ

I had a long walk, and I got tired. ᛁ·ᚺᚠᛗ·ᚠ·ᛚᛟᚷ·ᛈᚠᛚᚲ·ᚠᛏᛗ·ᛁ·ᚷᛟᛏ·ᛏᛁᚱᛗᛞ

Use your reference table to find the rune equivalent for the letters, write them out, then check if you got them right. Read back what you wrote to hear if it sounds right. Do this anytime you practice writing a word or sentence. Move on to a different word only after you are confident writing and reading the current one.

Meditation

To master runic divination, you'll need to connect with the energy of the runes. Meditation is a great way to get a sense of their energy and see which runes you might be drawn to and why. The symbolism related to the runes will be discussed in the next chapter, allowing you to discover more about why you may feel aligned with a specific rune. However, before you get to this part, you should spend a little time with the runes each day. That way, you'll be able to expand an understanding of their meanings from a conscious to an intuitive level, which you'll use in divination and magic. Learning the shapes of each rune, which aett they belong to, their English names, and symbolism before you start meditating with them is a good idea.

Choose a tranquil area where you won't be disturbed and prepare your body and mind for meditation. Wear comfortable clothes, and remove anything you might find constricting (including shoes, watch, jewelry, etc.). Sit in a relaxed position and take a few deep breaths to clear your mind from your daily preoccupations so that you can focus on the runes. Take a rune from your rune bag or box, and look at it for a few seconds. After this, close your eyes and imagine the rune standing tall in front of you. If you have trouble visualizing the runes this way, keep your eyes open and draw the shape of the rune with your hand in the air. Whichever method you choose, hold the rune in front of you and mentally retrace its outline.

Don't focus consciously on the meaning of the rune in front of you. Keep your attention on the rune's shape and concentrate on your intention of bonding with the rune. If your mind starts to wander, bring it back to the rune. Try to sense whether the rune is speaking to you and what the rune means to you in the present moment. Continue this for 15-30 minutes or until you can focus on this task. Repeat the following day with another rune until you go through them all.

Chapter 9: Runic Divination and Magic

Runes can be used for much more than just writing. This chapter will delve into how the runes were used for divination and other magical acts, including protection, assistance in spiritual growth, and much more. You'll also learn how Norse runes can be used for these purposes in modern times and what it takes to successfully master runic divination or magic.

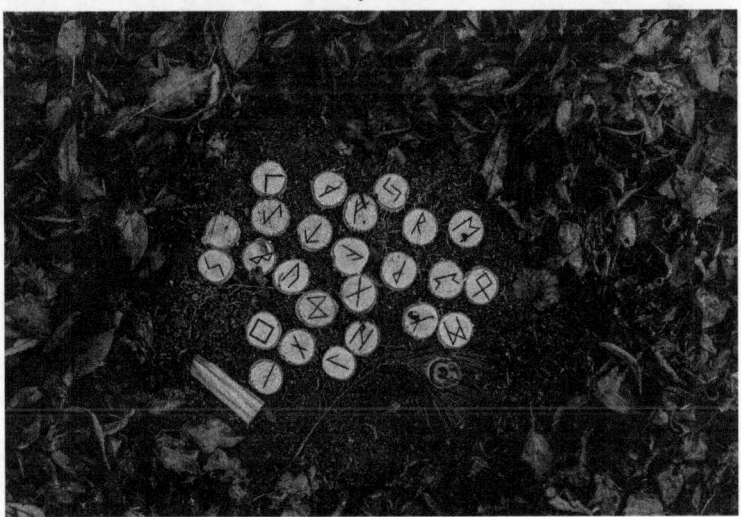

Runes can be used for much more than just writing.
https://www.pexels.com/photo/runic-letters-on-wood-chunks-and-ground-with-autumn-leaves-10110445/

Using Runes for Divination

According to the ancient Norse people, the runes held many secrets, including information about the future. This belief came from the myth in which Odin himself uses the runes to prophesize. The term "rune" comes from an Old English translation of an ancient Norse word, which means "secret." This also hints at the mystical nature of the runes. Originally the runes were small staves with the letters of the futhark inscribed into them. The staves were made from the branches of a nut-bearing tree and later from wood, stone, or bones. These were cast during a small, or more often, elaborate ritual, where the rune caster sought information about the future. The prophet offered a quick prayer to the gods, looked up towards the sky, and cast the runes on a white cloth in front of them. Then, they interpreted the results by relying on their vast knowledge and experience in runic symbolism.

Making Your Own Rune Kit

Nowadays, you can buy pre-made runes and entire rune-casting kits. The runes can be made from stone, wood, or even crystals. The latter carries different magical energy but can be infused with even more natural power. You can also make your own rune set. This would foster a stronger connection between your energy and the runes, making it easier for your intuition to pick up their meaning. It's also not very expensive, which is perfect for beginners, especially if you're just figuring out whether runic divination is the best fit for your needs.

Here are some ways to make your rune kit:

- **From wood:** Trees were known to have magical powers in Norse mythology, so making runes from wood is a great option to ensure that you're starting off with powerful tools. Branches of living trees are the best due to the high concentration of their essence. Make sure you ask the tree permission before cutting it and give thanks after you're done. You can paint the runes on the wood, but you can also carve them into the wood as a more durable option.
- **From stones:** If you're living near a beach or river, you'll find flat pebbles or rocks that are the perfect size for runes. These are more challenging to carve, but you can also paint the runes onto them and go over them with a clear protective coat to ensure that

the inscription won't wear off too quickly.

- **From clay:** The most manageable material to work with, but make sure to bake the clay staves properly. Otherwise, they'll easily chip and crack. Coat these as well after baking.

When you've chosen your material, make 24 runes to account for the 24 letters of the Elder Futhark. Some people make a blank rune too, but it's up to you to decide whether or not you want one. You can also make a couple of extra ones, just in case you make an error during painting and carving. Make sure that all the staves are similar in size and shape and that they are no bigger than what would comfortably fit in the palm of your hand. Then, you can move on to inscribing the runes by focusing your intention on the name of each one while you're creating them. When painting, you should ideally use red coloring. This resembles the color of blood, the substance the ancient Norse traditionally used to paint runes.

Consecrating Your Runes

After creating them, you'll need to consecrate your runes. This will help you connect with them before using them for divination. To do this, you'll need a strong focus, so ensure you aren't too preoccupied with other things. There are many consecration rituals for runes and other magical tools, but here is a simple one suitable for beginners:

- Place the runes in front of you and a candle beside them on your altar or table.
- Light the candle and focus on its flame while you take a few deep breaths to help you focus.
- Take a rune into your hands, recite its name aloud and start moving it over the flame.
- Lay the rune down apart from the rest, and repeat with the remaining symbols.
- When you're finished, put the runes in a protective bag or box to keep them away from negative influences until you need to use them.

Casting the Runes

There are many ways to cast and interpret the runes for divination. While the previous chapter has introduced several meanings for each rune, the symbolic meaning during a prophecy depends entirely on your interpretation. For example, Isa means "ice," which can be interpreted as being stuck. However, when it comes up, you'll need to wonder whether you feel stuck or not. Maybe your gut is telling you that you have to stop and wait for a better opportunity. If this is your first thought when looking at Isa, it's probably the correct meaning for you at the time. Don't second guess your intuition; listen to it.

You can choose to follow the ancient method and toss the runes on a cloth to interpret them. You can also use one of the modern methods, which involves laying out the runes in a specific pattern, similar to the Tarot card layouts. Practice interpreting one rune at a time by asking questions that can be answered with a "Yes" or "No." These will only confirm what you already know in your subconscious but will help you get the hang of listening to your intuition.

Once you've mastered reading one rune, you can move on to a three-rune spread. For this, you'll need to take a deep breath, take out three runes, and lay them in front of you in a horizontal line. The middle one reflects your current situation and actions, and the one on the left shows past influences. While the rune on the right illustrates the most likely future outcome of your present actions. Another layout, the four-rune cast, is very similar to this one. The only difference is that you'll lay out the runes in a circular pattern and have an additional rune indicating other people's influence on your future.

When you've become confident in casting and interpreting simple spreads, you can move on to the 5, 7, 9, or even 24-rune spreads. The latter uses all 24 runes to give you a full scope of the events you can expect in the coming year.

The Five-Rune Layout

- After relaxing, lay out the runes in the shape of a cross.
- The rune at the base of the cross indicates general influences regarding the answer to your question.
- The rune at the left arm of the cross showcases the negative forces affecting your future.
- The rune at the highest position alludes to the positive effects of current actions on future events.

- The rune at the right arm of the cross provides the most direct resolution to your inquiry or issue.
- The central rune represents future actions that will impact the answer to your inquiry.

The Spread of Seven Runes

- After clearing your mind with a deep breath, lay out seven runes in a V shape.
- The rune in the uppermost position on the left side indicates past events that can affect future outcomes.
- The next rune on the left represents the influence of your current actions or situation over future events.
- The last rune on the left side illuminates future behavior or events that may impact the answer to the inquiry.
- The rune at the base of the V tells you what to do to obtain the desired outcome.
- The first rune on the other side at the base of the V points to feelings that may impact your behavior.
- The rune above it shows hindrances and problems related to the inquiry.
- The last rune remaining indicates the most likely future developments associated with your inquiry.

A Simple Nine-Rune Cast

- Draw a deep breath and take nine runes from your rune bag or box while focusing on your question.
- Place the runes into your dominant hand.
- Closing your eyes, scatter the runes in front of you. Don't worry about how they land.
- Open your eyes and look at how the runes have landed.
- How many runes are facing up, and how many have landed face down? The ones facing up are influences you were already aware of and are likely interested in. The ones that landed face down are influences you weren't aware of.

- The runes that land close to the center represent the most significant influences you need to focus on. The ones towards the edge may have a lesser impact but shouldn't be disregarded either.

Using Runes for Magic

Other magical uses for runes included protection, love spells, talismans and charms, and bind runes. The latter involves combining two runes by writing and binding them together, letting them enhance each other's power. While these were less popular in ancient times, they are often used for different runic magic work in modern times. You can use them as sigils, amulets, or to enrich your spells and ask the deities for empowerment.

Here are some of the ways you can make bind runes:

- **Linear:** The runes are placed in the same line and used for several purposes.
- **Stacked:** The runes are placed onto the same axis, often used to represent reality.
- **Same stave:** Several runes are placed in a specific order along the same axis, used to eliminate a significant issue.
- **Radial:** Several runes share the same center point, perfect for defense magic as the runes are centering each other's power.

Runic spells, charms, and incantations were much more commonly used by the ancient Norse, and many are still in use today. These could be simple words, where one word has such a powerful effect that in itself is enough to take effect. An example of this would be the word "all," which has been found on amulets alongside Norse people's remains and was said to ward off evil spirits. Composite words were also used for inscriptions on charms, spells, and amulets. These were often used in elaborate rituals for fertility, protection, and summoning arches.

Sometimes complete spells were inscribed in the runic alphabet. One of these was the spells in which Odin was called upon to help find a thief:

"*I call on you, Odin, the mightiest of gods.*

Tell me the name of the person who stole from me.

Tell me now, who is taunting me so brazenly.

Show me, Odin. I call on you now.

I ask you to give the name of whoever stole.
And I thank you for your help."

Creating Your Own Charms and Spells

While you can use pre-existing charms and spells, creating your own would make them even more powerful. However, to do this, you'll need to understand how the position of the runes will impact their effectiveness in a charm or spell. Here are the positions to consider:

- **Direct position:** This works just like when a person stands directly in front of you so you can see their clear stance. This position of the runes indicates their most indicative values and symbolism. Use them to get straight to the point with your spell or charm.

- **Inverted runes:** These runes are influenced by a power that makes them behave differently. These are still related to the direct meaning of the runes but in a somewhat exaggerated version. They can come in handy when you need lots of power in your spell or charm.

- **Mirror position:** These runes are more powerful as they are created by other runes in the Elder Futhark. You can use them to make bind runes, but exercise precaution. If used incorrectly, they have the power to trap energy and provide very little in return. Some runes don't have a mirrored version, and these only are used for selfless actions.

Making your own spells and charms isn't the easiest task, especially if you're a novice. You'll need to work on your visualization technique and sharpen your intuition as much as possible. When creating a spell using runes, you'll need to visualize your intent, so it becomes a word you can see in front of you. The easier it is for you to do this, the more powerful your spell will be. An exercise that can help you learn how to visualize runes is simply picking one out from a table in front of you and trying to imagine it with your eyes closed. When you've mastered imagining the runes' shape, you can add textures or images to their forms. Try finding images that best represent their core meaning, and focus on these when trying to visualize them. This will help you memorize the details you'll need when trying to create the runes that best describe your intention.

Bind Runes

Forming bind runes will also require you to understand the essence of each individual rune. Some runes, when combined, develop a hidden meaning, which can affect the outcome of your spell or charm. Start practicing with a two-rune combination first, and make sure to have a short-term goal in mind while doing so. Analyze the two runes separately, consider their meaning, and contemplate what you want to achieve. Visualize your goals, and see if the runes will fit the purpose. If not, feel free to select runes with a meaning that's more aligned with your intention. Take your time with this step because some runes have multiple meanings.

Grab a pen and a piece of paper, and draw several combinations of the runes you've chosen. Don't worry about getting things right on the first try or even the tenth one. Just create whatever combination comes to your mind. When you think you have sufficient combinations, leave them for a while. Go finish an errand, or simply go for a walk. Sometimes the choice of the perfect rune will come to your mind while you're not focusing on it. If not, look at the sketches again and tap into your intuition to see which one you feel drawn to the most.

Next, depending on your purpose, select the material. If you have a long-term goal, you'll need something sturdy, like stone or wood. If you have a short-term goal, paper will also suffice. Don't forget to consider whether you want to create a spell, a talisman, or something else. For example, if you're making a protective charm for yourself, you'll need to carry it around to take effect. In this case, you can create a pendant for a necklace. However, if you need protection for your home, an art piece to hang on your walls would be a more suitable choice.

Carve or paint the bind rune in a calming atmosphere. You can meditate beforehand to relax your mind and let it focus on the task. You can repeat the meditation with your finished bind rune and thank your guides for their help. Keep the rune somewhere you can look at whenever you need to draw on its power.

Chapter 10: Galdr Magic

There are numerous misconceptions about the concept of Galdr. This false information is likely a result of how the practice was described in one of Edred Thorsson's books. The text suggested that it is the mere chanting of runes. Even though many people today practice Galdr this way, which is completely fine, it's not exactly how ancient Nordic people conducted this practice. That said, Galdr was primarily an oral tradition, which means that we have very little written evidence of this form of magic. After reading this chapter, you'll understand what Galdr is and learn about the history and origins of this magical practice. You'll also find out the uses of runes and Galdr and how to practice them. Finally, you'll come across a step-by-step guide on how to conduct the High-Seat Rite.

What Is Galdr?

Galdr is an Old Norse term from the Old English/High German word Galan, which means "singing incantations." The verb Galan means "to chant," and the Old English variation Galdor means "witchcraft/ spell."

Galdr is a type of Norse magic that is practiced by chanting or singing incantations. There are two patron deities of this practice, Odin and Sigyn. Odin is the ruler of countless affairs, including magic and war. He is considered the patron of Galdr because he mastered 18 of these incantations. Sigyn is the goddess of victory and the wife of Loki. She is known for being the fetter or goddess of Galdr.

The History of Galdr

Before we get into the history of Galdr, we must first explore the idea of runes. While runes are the letters of the old Germanic alphabet, they are also defined as "incantations" or "symbols that carry a mystical or mysterious significance."

The term "rune" originated from Germanic languages and dialects and came from a verb that means "to whisper" and was then adopted by the Celtic alphabet as a term that means "secret."

This definition was then used to describe a hieroglyphic or ideographic symbol of a unit of mysterious lore, which served as a token for timeless concepts. Later, this symbol was adopted into another writing system which appointed a certain phonetic value to each hieroglyphic symbol. In modern times, people mistakenly describe runes as just letters of the alphabet.

Only a few forms of runes have been used to represent phonetic symbols throughout history. These could be referred to as letter runes. However, the majority's use remained for ideographic purposes - glyph runes.

Letter runes mainly developed and standardized within the magical futhark runic alphabetical system. That said, glyph runes also played a major role in the creation of Elder Futhark.

Magicians and priests during the Bronze Age, and even earlier, developed ideographic symbols that captured the essence of their magical and spiritual practices and teachings. Countless rocks in Scandinavia have carvings of these graphic expressions. These holy symbols, often referred to as pre-runic signs, gave rise to letter and glyph runes.

Pre-runic signs were purely ideographic until they came in contact with Mediterranean cultures. Only then did Germanic peoples learn about the concept of symbolic representation of phonetics and language during around the 2nd century BCE.

Germanic peoples represented their phonetics with runes that somewhat resemble Greek, Etruscan, or Latin characters. This idea is particularly relevant to the creation of galdrar and highlights the practice's significance to particular runic forms.

The initial stage of the development of the runic system served as the framework for rune magic. At that time, these ideographs weren't available for public use. They were incorporated into magical number formulas and sounds, or galdrar, and were used to induce certain magical results. Soon after that, runes were publicly used to express the written forms of the Germanic language.

It should be noted that magical connotations were only minimal during these stages of runic development. However, all three ideographic, phonetic, and sound-formulaic runic formulations were used together and can all be incorporated into modern-day runic practices.

The Uses of Runes and Galdr

Runes can be incorporated into magical practices in a plethora of ways. However, in ancient times, talismanic magic was perhaps the most common rune magic method. This method requires practitioners to carve runes into numerous objects before imbuing them with psychic power. Doing so was thought to induce changes in the magician, or vitki, and their environment.

In the 44th chapter of the Egils Saga, which is a saga about Egill Skallagrímsson's clan, Egill worries that someone is trying to kill him by poisoning his drink. He inscribed runes on the horn that contained the drink and stabbed his hand to color the runes with blood. This causes the horn to shatter to release all the poison. Hundreds of runic talismans remain to this day and can be examined to gain a deeper understanding of the magic behind them.

There are generally two types of galdr - poetic runagaldrar, which refers to magical runic incantations, and stadhagaldr, which means posture incantation or magic. Poetic runagaldrar was also commonly practiced. The Poetic Edda, which is an Old Norse collection of anonymous narrative poems, uses the voice of several of these ancient runic magical incantations. The drinking horns of Gallehus serve as evidence for stadhagaldr. These drinking horns have several magical formulas inscribed on them. Many of them portray human-like figures standing in runic postures. It is believed that children were taught the alphabet by using stadhagaldr methods. They had children stand in poses that resembled each letter.

The Galdr is the basic form of a mantra or incantation. You can think of it as the rune's vibratory expression. Galdr is an indispensable tool to the vitki throughout all the phases of rune magic. It is the medium that allows the runic force to manifest itself. The Galdr formulae are highly adaptable and can be flexibly incorporated into several practices. This is why each practitioner must experiment with it. The simple sound Galdr, which we will be exploring in more depth, is the most basic and practical when it comes to conducting self-guided ritual work.

Methods of Practice

If you're conducting basic magic while working with runes, you can either use Galdr or Taufr. Like Galdr, a Taufr can be described as a talisman or incantation.

There are no existing records of how the ancient Norse practiced Galdr, but there are two popular ways to practice this art according to modern practices. Edred Thorsson mentions one of them in his book, where he explains that you can recite the Elder Futhark runes in the form of a sing-song. Doing so would help you raise your vibrational frequencies to meet the vibrations of the runes. Thorsson's method was believed to be inspired by Guido von Liszt, who sought out the chanting technique from Hindu practices. Hindus believe that certain words possess a unique set of attributes. When you put them together, you will come up with mantras that induce unique effects. Those Hindu chants are known as seed mantras.

Guido von Liszt made up his own version of this practice and applied it to Armanen runes. Bringing vowels and consonants together allows you to create a Galdr, which, like a seed mantra, generates a specific desired effect. Thorsson expanded on this concept by applying it to Elder Futhark. You can chant the combination of Futhark rune vowels and consonants to generate the Galdr.

If you wish to try out the other method, you would have to write up a poetic spell. This spell must make use of the symbolic meanings of the runes. You should also employ poetic devices in the process. These devices are mainly alliteration and kennings. After the spell is formulated, it is sung to generate the Galdr.

There isn't much that we know regarding the Taufr, except that it is a talisman that was inscribed into various materials found in nature. Magical practices were thought to be centered around it. The Taufr draws its power from the runes that are on it. The runes also determine the purpose of the Taufr.

Practicing Galdr

There were both male and female practitioners of Galdr. This was one of the very few Norse magical practices that people didn't call men who practiced it "unmanly." Surprisingly, some people considered it a manly form of magic. However, women who practiced it weren't considered any less feminine.

Since we don't have much evidence on how runes were historically incorporated into the practice of Galdr, it's fine if you wish to try your own take on the practice. Some incantations were completed in the Galdralag poetic meter, which was created for spells. While these incantations were more formal, informal methods were also used. Evidence suggests that Galdr was mainly based on creative wording and poetic language. It represents the intrinsic power of words.

Galdr was used in many instances. For instance, practitioners were thought to be able to induce storms, cast madness onto a person, cause faraway ships to sink, ease the process of childbirth, soften armor, decide which side emerges victorious in battle, and turn swords blunt.

Several poems in the Poetic Edda, such as Hávamál, reference Galdr. It was widely believed that Odin knew 18 Galdrar against numerous forces. The Edda also explained that the deity could bring the deceased to life.

The Galdralag Poetic Meter

Evidence suggests that Galdralag was only used for magical incantations. While most poetry today focuses on rhyming, Old Norse poetry emphasized alliteration, which commonly included tongue twisters. Alliteration is the repetition of sounds at the start of words. Ancient Norse poetry also focused on the use of kennings, which are similar to metaphors. Complex kennings are often very hard to grasp.

Ljoðaháttr, which is the poetic meter of chants, and Galdralag are much alike. While the former is composed of a total of six lines, Galdralag contains seven lines. Ljoðaháttr includes a line that is paired with alliteration, followed by a line that's unpaired. This means that lines 1 and 2 and 4 and 5 are paired, while 3 and 6 are unpaired. A Galdralag follows the same structure, in addition to a 7th unpaired line, which emphasizes the one before it.

You only need one alliterated word in each of the paired lines in Galdralag. However, it's fine if you wish to add more. The unpaired lines must have at least two alliterated words each.

Many practitioners frown upon the modern version of Galdr, which was created by Edred Thorsson, because it only requires you to repeat the name of the Futhark. They suggest that it lacks any substance and may even be disrespectful to the original, ancient practice. While some of their arguments make sense, we believe that the modern version of Galdr is an acceptable form of practice.

This table only includes the first 4 futhark names to give you an insight into their symbolic meanings and the phonetic values that they represent:

Name	Phonetic Value	Symbol
Fehu	F	Mobile force, energy, power, fertility, destruction, creation
Uruz	U, V	Health, strength, organic organization, wealth
Thurisaz	Th	Power of defense and destruction, action, the regeneration that follows destruction, applied power
Ansuz	A	Expression, transformation, ecstasy, inspiration, death mystery

High-Seat Rite: Step-By-Step Guide

This rite is one of the most common Norse rituals that combine divination and singing spells.

You'll Need the following:
- An offering
- A High Seat
- A cloak
- A drum
- A staff

Before you start, you will need to invite at least 8 people over to conduct the ritual with you, as these are the roles that you need to fill:

- **The Seer:** The person who travels to Helheim
- **The Master of Ceremonies:** The one responsible for directing the rite
- **The watcher/watchers:** The person or people observing the ritual
- **The battery:** The people responsible for raising the energy
- **The chorus:** The ones who sing and invite spirits over
- **The audience:** The ones responsible for asking the questions

You must also purify your space before conducting your ritual. In that case, you'll want to cast a protective circle and invoke the deity you wish to work with, Hel, Odin, or Freyja. You should always ask Hel permission to enter Helheim, as it's her realm. If you believe that the answer you received is "no," don't proceed with the rite under any circumstances.

If she grants you permission to enter Helheim, you should start building up the energy you need for your rite. Get everyone involved in the process, as raising the energy should be done through drumming and dancing ecstatically. Once you're done, sit and gather around in a circle and start calling on your ancestors and spirit to join you.

The Master of Ceremonies should ask everyone to visualize the world tree floating right in the middle of the space. They should also instruct everyone to chant Galdr and the Vardlokkur, which are protective chants that help you call on healing spirits and guardians beforehand. The whole group should be putting some physical input into the rite, whether they're clapping, moving, or influencing the rite in some other way. Up to this moment, all the work put into the rite is aimed at readying the Seer.

Once the Seer feels like they're well-prepared, they should take the cloak and staff. The Master of the Ceremonies should pay attention to the Seer, as they're the one who'll determine when it's time for the Seer to walk the path. Once everyone quietens down, the Master of the Ceremonies should guide the Seer through. They'll direct the Seer via visualization and ask them to imagine themselves in a field surrounded by soft soil. The Seer should visualize himself sinking into the cool soil below their feet.

The Master of the Ceremonies should then physically guide the Seer to walk into a spiral. This spiral is symbolic of the Yggdrasil. Then, the Master of Ceremonies should guide the Seer, via visualization, through the path-walking experience as they travel to Helheim. They should then be guided to the High Chair, where they'll describe everything they see. The Master of Ceremonies should avoid calling the Seer by name as they guide them through the questions. Even though this is their role, addressing them by it will only break them from their trance state. When the Master of Ceremonies is done asking the questions, the Seer should leave Helheim and then be called by their name. This will bring them back. They should remove the cloak, and everyone should stop the music. The offerings should be provided before giving thanks to bring the rite to an end.

Now that you have read this chapter, you know everything you need about the history and uses of Galdr magic. While very little is known about how this form of magic was practiced among ancient Norse peoples, you can still explore the modern renditions of the practice.

Conclusion

The concepts of Norse mythology that have been passed down to us are quite misleading and even nuanced in some ways. The sources of these stories and history are countless, and many of them paint very different pictures of Viking history and mythology. While these sources have provided us with a range of information concerning the Norse world, its beliefs, and the stories of the otherworld, there are considerable pieces missing and altered from these legendary tales.

We have an immensely vibrant and vivid image of the Norse culture, history, spirituality, and mythology, but we are far from understanding the full story. Unsurprisingly, considering how long it has been, there is no course that we can take to fill these gaps. Understandably, many people who deem Norse and Viking history and spirituality important have tried to fill these missing pieces with two approaches.

They undertake heaps of literature and scholarly research to understand how the history played out and what the origin stories of Norse mythology were. This method definitely produces more esteemed and credible sources of information. However, the unavailability of sufficient literature is a serious obstacle to this approach. An alternative solution to the problem of missing information is through creative imagination. Many authors use this method to create stories and assume historical events through imagination and mere common sense.

Plus, contrary to what many people think, there's nothing actually methodologically wrong with this approach unless you're writing for an audience that demands an extreme level of thoroughness when it comes to research. After all, that's what the Vikings themselves used to do. In fact, many authors back then did the exact same thing. Why do you imagine we have so many variations in the telling of these stories? It's because the people who were narrating these stories in the past constantly added new elements to these tales.

Many would add, subtract, and alter the happenings in these myths and even in actual history. Ultimately, this is how living traditions are passed down from generation to generation. They're not fossils that need to be mindlessly passed over the same way again and again. They constantly change and evolve with time and norms. After all, no tradition can live on without a little alteration and innovation.

As such, Norse history, culture and mythology were thoroughly infused with this view, and people today are fully aware of this. However, it does not lessen their interest in the subject. If anything, it makes their thirst for knowledge even more. If you're one of these people, hopefully, the contents of this book have quenched your thirst for knowledge regarding Norse traditions, culture, religion, and mythology.

If you're still buzzing with questions, a whole world of information is available for you online. Ultimately, Norse culture and mythology are a rich part of history. The gods were pillars who held everything together by tirelessly defending and fighting for this world. This attitude was adopted by the Viking races so unflinchingly strong. All this left an abundance of stories and myths for you to learn from.

Glossary: Norse Terms

Aesir
This is the classification of Gods mentioned in Scandinavian culture or Norse mythology. They were warrior deities who resided in Asgard. They were in opposition to Vanir, who were considered to be older deities associated with earth. Though there are varied mentions of Aesir deities in literature, this list usually includes Odin, Freya, Thor, Loki, Tui, Balder, Vali, Odinir, Brag, and Hoenir.

Altar
A designated flat space exclusively used for worship, magical practice, and religious customs.

Asatru
The contemporary reestablishment of Germanic paganism is dedicated to the old deities of Norse mythology.

Ax
The Ax holds a special meaning in Norse symbolism. It was not just a common weapon used by the Vikings but also considered a holy sign.

Balder
The son of Odin, and Freya, Balder was one of the purest Aesir deities. His mother made everything in the world swear an oath not to harm him, except for mistletoe. The trickster god Loki used this exception to kill him.

Balefire

A special fire lit for magical practices or traditional festivals like Beltane, Yule, Samhain, or Midsummer.

Berserker

Considered to be a legendary Norse champion, Berserker was known for his savage and reckless nature during battle.

Bifrost

The inter-cosmic bridge connecting different realms to Asgard. It is usually depicted as a giant rainbow bridge. It is mainly said to connect Asgard and Midgard.

Blot

A sacrifice or offering presented to the Gods or other deities common in Germanic Paganism and Neopaganism. This offering is usually in the form of a feast.

Cauldron

A large pot in spell work and rituals in Norse magic practices. Cauldrons represent the Goddess and water of rebirth.

Centering

The process of grounding your energy before rituals. This is usually done through meditation or other similar techniques.

Casting Circle

A casting circle refers to an area of sacred space that has been consecrated for use in worship. This space is typically referred to as a "ring of stones," and it is typically used by practitioners of the Norse religion or heathenism. Casting circles have deep roots in Norse culture and tradition, with many examples of these sacred spaces left throughout Northern Europe. One of the most commonly-known examples comes from the island of Öland in Sweden, where archaeologists have discovered more than 80 rings dating back thousands of years.

Cleansing

The process of eliminating negative energy from an object or surrounding space.

Dis

A spirit or deity associated with fate or fertility. These spirits can be both benevolent and spiteful toward humans.

Divination
The art of gathering information from the collective unconsciousness or universal guides. The process can be aided with the help of divination tools and techniques.

Dwarf
Mythical creatures that are skilled in metalwork and mining.

Elf
A supernatural being mentioned in many myths and stories. Elves are delicate, magical creatures with pointy ears.

Esbat
A Norse ritual that takes place during a full moon.

Fylgja
According to Norse mythology, Fylgia is a magical creature that accompanies people. This creature usually appears in the form of an animal and is believed to be a true reflection of the person's character or soul.

Galdr
The Norse word for incantation or spell. This was usually practiced in combination with rituals by both men and women.

Grounding
The process of dispelling any extra energy produced after a magical ritual by dissipating it into the earth. This process is also done to center oneself before a ritual.

Hammer
The hammer is not just a tool used in Norse culture but is also a representation. It is the symbol of Thor and a tool that can be used to create and destroy. Hammer charms were often worn for protection.

Havamal
A renowned poem that is included in the great Poetic Edda. The Poetic Edda is a collection of many Norse poems dating all the way back to the ancient Norse civilization. Havamal itself is a collection of different poems combined together.

Hel
Hel is the underworld of Norse mythology and the name of the Goddess who ruled it. Writers often use the name Hela so that the two

won't be confused. According to some legends, Hela was the daughter of Loki, the trickster God. Some myths claim that she was rotting flesh and nothing else from the waist down. Hel, the underworld, was just as dreadful. It was a place where the people who died from sickness would go.

Herbalism

The art of utilizing herbs and plants to heal and treat diseases. It was a very prevalent technique in Norse history.

Jotunn

Roughly translated to giant, the Jotunn in Norse mythology are a race of spirits of nature who have superhuman powers. Legend suggests that they usually stand in opposition to the Aesir and Vanir.

Libation

The offering is presented to a deity, spirit, or ghost as part of a ritual.

Loki

The mischievous trickster god, Loki, was often confused as the God of evil. Norse mythology depicts him as the father of Hela and Fenrir. According to older legends, Loki planned Balder's death, for which he was punished by being bound to a rock until Ragnarök, a major event in Norse mythology.

Mead

A famous drink in Norse mythology, mead is a combination of fermented honey and water. It was usually served in Valhalla to the warriors after they had had a long day of fighting and training.

Norns

The Norns were the three virgin goddesses of fate and destiny; they were said to sit beneath the tree of life and spin the webs of destiny.

Oath

A formal promise or agreement, usually through invoking a divine entity as a witness, regarding one's intentions or future behavior.

Odin

The major God in Norse mythology, Odin, is a famous deity known by almost everyone. He was the inspiration for many famous poems in Norse history.

Poetic Edda
A very famous collection of pre-historic poems from the Norse age. It is one of the primary sources of Norse mythology.

Runes
Ancient letters used by Norse people. They were used for various purposes, including writing, magic rituals, and divination. People who didn't have writing systems saw the runes themselves as magic.

Runecasting
Rune casting is a divination technique used to obtain guidance from your subconscious mind. While many people argue that the source of guidance is divine, it's actually your subconscious mind guiding you toward the correct choice.

Sabbat
The eight Wiccan celebrations are meant to celebrate seasonal transitions. These include Imbolc, Ostara, Beltane, Litha, Lughnasadh, Mabon, Samhain, and Yule.

Seidr
The ancient term for sorcery was practiced back in the late Scandinavian iron age in Norse society. Many scholars and historians have argued over the nature of this practice. They ultimately agreed that it was shamanic and involved visual journeys.

Skald
A word of ancient Norse culture, it roughly translates to poet. It was used to refer to a court poet or bard from the ninth century onwards. Skald was a reciter and composer of legendary poems paying tribute to the brave heroes and their deeds. The accomplishment of being a successful composer was regarded as highly as being a warrior.

Spell
A magical practice that is non-religious in nature. It is done by speaking words, chanting, and gesturing. A spell should be clear, concise, and done with genuine intent.

Spirit
There are many meanings associated with the word spirit, but most of them relate it to a non-corporeal being. This word is also often used to refer to someone's personality, consciousness, or soul. Spirits can also be the surviving notion of a deceased person.

Stadhagaldr

A type of runic yoga famous in Norse history. The gestures and postures are similar to the magical form of the runes.

Sword

Another weapon commonly used in ancient Norse civilizations. The sword was a symbol of nobility and bravery. It was considered to be the embodiment of one's family legacy.

Talisman

A sacred object used to attract a specific kind of energy or force to its owner.

Teutonic

The ancient language of the Germanic Norse civilizations.

Troll

Another supernatural creature with a distinct appearance is mentioned frequently in Norse mythology. Trolls were either depicted as giants or dwarfs. They were said to live in small family units in caves or mountains.

Valhalla

Valhalla was the sacred place designated for fallen warriors who died heroically in battle. This place was depicted as a stunning palace of spears with a ceiling made out of shields. Considered to be presided over by Odin, Valhalla was the afterlife for brave warriors.

Valkyries

The Valkyries were the ones who took the fallen warriors into Valhalla. Their name translates to choosers of the slain. These beings were considered to be fate weavers and often took on the role of the Norse Norns.

Vanir

The Vanir were another group of deities in Norse mythology associated with fertility and nature. They were also associated with youth, luck, health, and magic.

Völva

A powerful seer and prophetess, Volva was a female magic practitioner in the ancient Norse society. She was able to foretell events of the future and provide warnings. According to a famous myth, Odin called Volva from the dead, only to have her tell him how the world would end.

Yggdrasil

Yggdrasil is also commonly known as the tree of life in many Norse legends. It has played a central role in many legendary stories. According to one legend, the nine realms came into existence around this mythical tree.

Here's another book by Silvia Hill that you might like

Free Bonus from Silvia Hill available for limited time

Hi Spirituality Lovers!

My name is Silvia Hill, and first off, I want to THANK YOU for reading my book.

Now you have a chance to join my exclusive spirituality email list so you can get the ebooks below for free as well as the potential to get more spirituality ebooks for free! Simply click the link below to join.

P.S. Remember that it's 100% free to join the list.

$27 FREE BONUSES

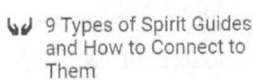 9 Types of Spirit Guides and How to Connect to Them

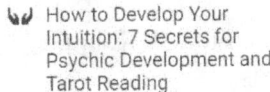 How to Develop Your Intuition: 7 Secrets for Psychic Development and Tarot Reading

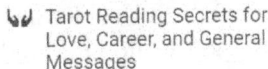 Tarot Reading Secrets for Love, Career, and General Messages

Access your free bonuses here
https://livetolearn.lpages.co/paganism-paperback/

References

The Current Chief, The Former Chief, & Patroness, O. (2019, November 27). What is Druidry ? Order of Bards, Ovates & Druids; OBOD. https://druidry.org/druid-way/what-druidry

Cartwright, M. (2021). Ancient Celts. World History Encyclopedia. https://www.worldhistory.org/celt/

Jarus, O. (2014, May 20). Who were the Druids? Livescience.com; Live Science.

Patrick, S. (2017, November 30). Who were Celts. HISTORY. https://www.history.com/topics/ancient-history/celts

The Celts. (n.d.). Ibiblio.org. https://www.ibiblio.org/gaelic/celts.html

The history behind Ireland's ancient Druids. (2021, December 5). Irishcentral.com. https://www.irishcentral.com/roots/history/history-Irelands-ancient-Druids

Who were the Druids? (2017, March 21). Historic UK. https://www.historic-uk.com/HistoryUK/HistoryofWales/Druids

An introduction to Druidry. (2017, October 8). The Druids Garden. https://thedruidsgarden.com/2017/10/08/an-introduction-to-druidry/

Bard, D. (2019, December 27). The gift of the Four Treasures. The Highland Bard. https://www.morgynbard.com/post/the-gift-of-the-four-treasures

Common practice and beliefs within Druidry. (2013, May 11). The Druid Network. https://druidnetwork.org/what-is-druidry/beliefs-and-definitions/articles/common-practice-and-beliefs-within-druidry/

Cosmology. (n.d.). Unc.edu https://exploringcelticciv.web.unc.edu/cosmology/

Four magical treasures of Tuatha DE Danann. (2018, April 7). Ancient Pages.

https://www.ancientpages.com/2018/04/07/four-magical-treasures-of-tuatha-de-danann/

I. E. (2022, May 27). What's the difference between a bard, a vate, and a druid? Irish Myths. https://irishmyths.com/2022/05/27/bards-vs-vates-vs-druids/

Land, sky, sea: Elements from a druid perspective. (2016, May 27). WitchPetals. https://witchpetals.wordpress.com/2016/05/27/land-sky-sea-elements-from-a-druid-perspective/

Maguire, L. (n.d.). Pantheism. Philosophy Talk https://www.philosophytalk.org/blog/pantheism

Phillips, M. A. (2012, July 8). Living in land, sky, and sea. Author M. A. Phillips. https://ditzydruid.com/2012/07/08/living-in-land-sky-and-sea/

Tauseef, K. (2022, March 1). What is the Real Celtic Creation Myth? Ancient Origins. https://www.ancient-origins.net/human-origins-folklore/celtic-creation-myth-0016475/

The 6 core principles of the GMDO. (n.d.). Greenmountaindruidorder.org. https://greenmountaindruidorder.org/the-gmdo/the-6-core-principles-of-the-gmdo/

The Current Chief, The Former Chief, & Patroness, O. (2019a, November 27). Druid beliefs. Order of Bards, Ovates & Druids; OBOD. https://druidry.org/druid-way/beliefs

The Current Chief, The Former Chief, & Patroness, O. (2019b, November 27). Ethics in Druidry. Order of Bards, Ovates & Druids; OBOD. https://druidry.org/druid-way/ethics-in-druidry

Nomads, T. (2022, March 21). Norse paganism for beginners: Quick introduction + resources. Time Nomads | Your Pagan Store Online. https://www.timenomads.com/norse-paganism-for-beginners/

A guide to Norse gods and goddesses - center of excellence. (2018, October 29). Centreofexcellence.com. https://www.centreofexcellence.com/norse-gods-goddesses/

About: Norse cosmology. (n.d.). DBpedia. https://dbpedia.org/page/Norse_cosmology

Apel, T. (2020a, August 2). Freya. Mythopedia. https://mythopedia.com/topics/freya

Apel, T. (2020b, August 3). Loki. Mythopedia. https://mythopedia.com/topics/loki

Apel, T. (2020c, August 3). Thor. Mythopedia. https://mythopedia.com/topics/thor

Christensen, C. (2020, October 8). This is why Odin sacrificed his eye in Norse mythology. Scandinavia Facts. https://scandinaviafacts.com/this-is-why-odin-sacrificed-his-eye/

Cruz, C. (2018, March 16). Yggdrasil, the Norse world tree. Tales by Trees. https://www.talesbytrees.com/yggdrasil-the-norse-world-tree/

Dan. (2012a, November 14). Cosmology. Norse Mythology for Smart People. https://norse-mythology.org/cosmology/

Dan. (2012b, November 15). Mimir. Norse Mythology for Smart People. https://norse-mythology.org/gods-and-creatures/others/mimir/

Dan. (2012c, November 15). Niflheim. Norse Mythology for Smart People. https://norse-mythology.org/cosmology/the-nine-worlds/niflheim/

Dan. (2012d, November 15). The Aesir-Vanir War. Norse Mythology for Smart People. https://norse-mythology.org/tales/the-aesir-vanir-war/

Dan. (2012e, November 15). Yggdrasil. Norse Mythology for Smart People. https://norse-mythology.org/cosmology/yggdrasil-and-the-well-of-urd/

Mark, J. J. (2018). Nine realms of Norse cosmology. World History Encyclopedia. https://www.worldhistory.org/article/1305/nine-realms-of-norse-cosmology/

Norse cosmology. (2021, May 12). Mythopedia. https://mythopedia.com/topics/norse-cosmology

Scott, J. (2020, December 3). A beginner's guide to Norse mythology. Life in Norway. https://www.lifeinnorway.net/norse-mythology/

Seven of the most important gods and goddesses in Norse mythology. (n.d.). Sky HISTORY TV Channel. https://www.history.co.uk/articles/seven-of-the-most-important-gods-and-goddesses-in-norse-mythology

The Editors of Encyclopedia Britannica. (2022). Odin. In Encyclopedia Britannica.

The mythological world of the Vikings. (n.d.). Historiska.Se. https://historiska.se/norse-mythology/mythological-world-of-the-vikings/

Apel, T. (2020, August 3). Fólkvangr. Mythopedia. https://mythopedia.com/topics/folkvangr

Dan. (2012a, November 14). Ancestors. Norse Mythology for Smart People. https://norse-mythology.org/gods-and-creatures/ancestors/

Dan. (2012b, November 14). Valkyries. Norse Mythology for Smart People. https://norse-mythology.org/gods-and-creatures/valkyries/

Dan. (2012c, November 15). Death and the Afterlife. Norse Mythology for Smart People. https://norse-mythology.org/concepts/death-and-the-afterlife/

Dan. (2012d, November 15). Hel (The Underworld). Norse Mythology for Smart People. https://norse-mythology.org/cosmology/the-nine-worlds/helheim/

Dan. (2012e, November 15). Valhalla. Norse Mythology for Smart People. https://norse-mythology.org/cosmology/valhalla/

Debutify. (n.d.). The Death and The Afterlife in Norse Mythology. VikingsBrandTM. https://www.vikingsbrand.co/blogs/norse-news/the-death-and-the-afterlife-in-norse-mythology

DK Find Out! (n.d.). DK Find Out! https://www.dkfindout.com/us/history/vikings/viking-warriors/

Mark, J. J. (2018). Norse ghosts & the afterlife. World History Encyclopedia. https://www.worldhistory.org/article/1290/norse-ghosts--the-afterlife/

Morgan, T. (2017, July 20). How did the Vikings honor their dead? HISTORY. https://www.history.com/news/how-did-the-vikings-honor-their-dead

Sogani, G. (2022, September 15). The idea of death and Hel in Norse mythos. Wondrium Daily. https://www.wondriumdaily.com/the-idea-of-death-and-hel-in-norse-mythos/

Tetrault, S., & BA. (2020, March 29). What's the Norse, or Viking, afterlife supposed to be like? Joincake.com. https://www.joincake.com/blog/norse-afterlife/

What can a Patronus say about a character? (2018, July 26). Wizardingworld.com; Wizarding World Digital. https://www.wizardingworld.com/features/what-can-a-patronus-say-about-a-character

Ásatrú and heathenry, belief and beards, racists and reporters. (n.d.). Norsemyth.org. https://www.norsemyth.org/2019/01/asatru-and-heathenry-belief-and-beards.html

Blain, J., & Wallis, R. J. (2009). Heathenry. In Handbook of Contemporary Paganism (pp. 413–432). BRILL.

Dan. (2012, November 15). Shamanism. Norse Mythology for Smart People. https://norse-mythology.org/concepts/shamanism

arithharger. (2015, September 4). Norse Shamanism. Whispers of Yggdrasil. https://arithharger.wordpress.com/2015/09/04/norse-shamanism/

The Return of the Völva: Recovering the Practice of Seiðr. (2012, February 15). Seidh.Org. https://seidh.org/articles/seidh/

Dan. (2012, November 15). Seidr. Norse Mythology for Smart People. https://norse-mythology.org/concepts/seidr/

Silver. (n.d.). Nordic Wiccan. Blogspot.Com. http://nordicwiccan.blogspot.com/2014/10/seidr.html

Circle-casting basics: All you need to know about magick circles. (n.d.). Grove and Grotto. https://www.groveandgrotto.com/blogs/articles/circle-casting-basics-all-you-need-to-know-about-magick-circles

Silver. (n.d.). Nordic Wiccan. Blogspot.Com. http://nordicwiccan.blogspot.com/2014/08/circle.html

Høst, A. [UCfgfjfS3huQ5mtaaZhsZDAg]. (2022, April 13). SEIDR 7:8 - The Craft in Seiðr. Youtube. https://www.youtube.com/watch?v=yF3H6xbWKkI

Høst, A. [UCfgfjfS3huQ5mtaaZhsZDAg]. (2022, April 27). SEIDR 8:8 - Planting our Staff in our own Turf. Youtube. https://www.youtube.com/watch?v=DuXF4Djc0kc&list=TLPQMTUxMDIwMjIg9ubefND5Ng&index=1

Dan. (2012a, November 14). The Vanir Gods and Goddesses. Norse Mythology for Smart People. https://norse-mythology.org/gods-and-creatures/the-vanir-gods-and-goddesses/

Dan. (2012b, November 15). Freyja. Norse Mythology for Smart People.

Dan. (2012c, November 15). Shamanism. Norse Mythology for Smart People. https://norse-mythology.org/concepts/shamanism/

Dan. (2014, November 3). Odr (god). Norse Mythology for Smart People. https://norse-mythology.org/odr-god/

Dowdeswell, M. (2022, September 17). The story, symbols and powers of Freyja, the Norse goddess of love. Ancient Origins

Freyja the goddess of love in Norse mythology. (n.d.). Bartleby.com. https://www.bartleby.com/essay/Freyja-The-Goddess-Of-Love-In-Norse-PCJEXC76JG

Inner Tapestry. (2018, October 17). Seiðstafr: The Norse shaman's staff of power. The HeartGlow Center. https://www.heartglowcenter.com/post/sei%C3%B0stafr-the-norse-shaman-s-staff-of-power

Norse shamanism: A Völva and her prophecies were feared among Norse gods and Vikings. (2020, May 19). Ancient Pages. https://www.ancientpages.com/2020/05/19/norse-shamanism-volva-prophecies-feared-among-norse-gods-vikings/

The return of the völva: Recovering the practice of seiðr. (2012, February 15). Seidh.org. https://seidh.org/articles/seidh/

Útiseta: The Norse shaman's wilderness quest. (2016, May 16). Shamamabear's Blog. https://shamamabear.wordpress.com/2016/05/16/utiseta-the-norse-shamans-wilderness-quest/

Viking archaeology. (n.d.). Archeurope.Info. http://viking.archeurope.info/index.php?page=seidr

Winquist, A. (2020, May 14). Meditation for protection with goddess Freyja —. The Soul Institute for Quantum Living.

Liam. (2022, January 23). Yggdrasil. Norse Mythology & Viking History. https://vikingr.org/norse-cosmology/yggdrasil-world-tree

Yggdrasil: The sacred ash tree of Norse mythology. (n.d.). The Public Domain Review https://publicdomainreview.org/collection/yggdrasil-the-sacred-ash-tree-of-norse-mythology

Dan. (2012, November 15). Ragnarok. Norse Mythology for Smart People. https://norse-mythology.org/tales/ragnarok/

Rhys, D. (2020, August 5). Yggdrasil symbol – origins and meaning. Symbol Sage. https://symbolsage.com/yggdrasil-symbol-meaning/

HeritageDaily. (2018, August 2). Yggdrasil and the 9 Norse worlds. HeritageDaily - Archaeology News; HeritageDaily. https://www.heritagedaily.com/2018/08/yggdrasil-and-the-9-norse-worlds/121244

Mark, J. J. (2018). Nine realms of Norse cosmology. World History Encyclopedia. https://www.worldhistory.org/article/1305/nine-realms-of-norse-cosmology/

www.ingramcontent.com/pod-product-compliance
Lightning Source LLC
Chambersburg PA
CBHW070327010526
44107CB00004B/442